An Integrated Approach to Resort Development

SIX CASE STUDIES

By Edward Inskeep and Mark Kallenberger

WORLD TOURISM ORGANIZATION

OMT • WTO • BTO

1992

First Edition

Cover Photo: Jameos de Agua, Lanzarote, Canary Islands, Spain; Cabildo Insular de Lanzarote.

Photo Credits:

INDONESIA: Bali Tourism Development Corporation.
KOREA: Korean National Tourism Corporation, Kyongju Tourism Agency.
MEXICO: Fondo Nacional de Fomento al Turismo.
DOMINICAN REPUBLIC: Oficina de Turismo de la República Dominicana de Madrid.
TURKEY: Turkish Ministry of Tourism.
SPAIN: Cabildo Insular de Lanzarote and Instituto de Turismo de España.

ISBN 92-844-0040-6

Depósito Legal: M. 38.375-1992

Printed in Spain

WORLD TOURISM ORGANIZATION
CALLE CAPITAN HAYA, 42
28020 MADRID, SPAIN
TEL: 571 06 28 FAX: 5713733 TELEX: 42188 OMT E

ACKNOWLEDGEMENTS

WTO and the authors would like to thank the tourism authorities in each resort and country for their cooperation. This publication could not have been produced without their assistance. Also thanks should be extended to Nancy Cockerell, Scott Wayne and Michael Berggren for editing, copyediting and proofreading this manuscript.

FIGURES

CONTENTS

Foreword

Key, Conclusions & Recommendations

FOREWORD

Over the last two decades, a number of large tourist resorts have been developed around the world, many of which have become highly popular holiday destinations. The growth in tourism generated by these resorts has brought significant economic and social benefits to their respective countries, including increased foreign exchange earnings, direct and indirect employment. In addition, the resorts' development has stimulated local and regional development, encouraging new local industries and international trade.

The success of these resorts can be largely attributed to the adoption of an integrated approach to their development — careful planning and implementation that took into consideration regional environmental, economic and socio-cultural factors. This kind of approach helps minimise environmental, socio-economic and marketing problems often associated with uncontrolled tourism development.

In line with WTO's concern for sustainable tourism development, a detailed evaluation of six tourist resorts was commissioned in 1990. The results of these case studies highlight the importance of an integrated approach to tourism development and offer some valuable lessons for tourism policy-makers and public and private sector planners. Many aspects of the approach to each resort's development are applicable to tourism resort projects all over the world.

Antonio Enríquez-Savignac
Secretary General
World Tourism Organization

KEY CONCLUSIONS & RECOMMENDATIONS

Conclusions

- If a resort is well planned, developed, marketed and managed, it can be very profitable in itself and also bring significant economic and social benefits to the region in which it is located, with foreign exchange and other benefits accruing to the central government.

- An integrated approach to resort development helps prevent the serious environmental, socio-economic and marketing problems often associated with unplanned tourism destinations.

Recommendations

- The development of an adequate infrastructure for resorts is essential, in order to maintain environmental quality and offer acceptable tourism services.

- Application of specific land use, development and design standards is also necessary to maintain the resort's character and quality.

- Resorts need to provide a wide range of tourist facilities, attractions and services, both within the resort environment and in the surrounding region, in order to maintain visitor satisfaction levels and diversify market sources.

- A high quality of tourism product and services is essential from the outset, and this should be maintained through continued good management and application of development and operational standards.

- Planning for later stages of development in a resort should be kept flexible to allow for changing market circumstances, but any modifications need to respect the resort's basic concept.

- Resort development must take into consideration employee training and the provision of housing and community services for employees and their families.

- The resort should be planned within its regional context, ideally with national or regional planning carried out first. Regional infrastructure and other improvements are often required as part of the resort development project.

- Adequate access to the resort and its region is essential to attract the desired tourist markets. Detailed planning of the area surrounding the resort, or even the entire region in which the resort is located, is necessary to guide future development that may take place as a result of the resort's impetus to tourism growth.

- Special organisational structures, with effective leadership and a competent technical staff, are necessary to develop and manage resorts. A high level of coordination is required between the many different agencies involved in a resort's development, as well as between the public and private sectors. This organisational structure, after gaining experience in the initial resort development, can often be used to develop other resorts in the country or region.

- Adequate financing is required for the resort and related regional infrastructure, which can be expensive to develop, as well as for the superstructure of accommodation and other facilities. Various financing techniques and sources are available, and approaches can be used to recover at least some of the infrastructure investment.

- Since a newly developing resort is an untested economic venture, the government or a public corporation may need to be pioneers in developing the first hotels, to encourage private investment.

- Marketing is essential, both to attract investors and also tourists to the resort.

Chapter 1

INTRODUCTION

Sustainable tourism development is one of the major issues facing the world's travel and tourism industry in the 1990s. Not only are tourists becoming more concerned about different forms of environmental pollution in their holiday destinations; there is also a growing number of tangible examples of environmental pollution translated into a loss of tourism income. The decline in popularity of certain traditional Mediterranean holiday resorts that have been overbuilt and under-maintained, the reduced appeal of the Black Forest damaged by acid rain, or the blooms of algae along the Adriatic coast of Italy are dramatic proof of the threat to tourism from environmental neglect.

The costs are impossible to quantify, but they are enormous. And it is already clear that tourists are beginning to shun operators and destinations that have received bad publicity over their environmental record. Leading tour operators themselves are increasingly appointing Environmental Advisors to monitor the environmental practices of hotels and resorts to avoid losing valuable clients.

As far as new resort development is concerned, the problems are perhaps less acute — but only on the condition that concerted efforts are made on the part of both governments and the operating sector to ensure an integrated approach to the resort's development. Only in this way will the development be sustainable and avoid placing undue strains on the carrying capacity of the resort or the destination.

An *'integrated approach to resort development'* implies the controlled planning and implementation of resort projects in order to achieve a balanced development that satisfies economic, environmental and social objectives. In general, it applies to long term project development — at times, over a period of many years — and constant monitoring and control at the different phases of development ensure that the basic concept can be adapted to changing circumstances and market demand.

The success of an integrated tourist resort depends on a number of factors. These include a good transportation infrastructure with easy access to and within the resort for guests and staff, and an architectural design that blends into the surrounding natural environment, reflecting traditional local designs and using as many local materials as possible. Specific natural geographical attractions should be preserved and incorporated into the resort wherever feasible, and it needs adequate utility services, such as water supply, electric power, telecommunications, sewage and solid waste disposal systems.

Successful integrated resorts are also planned within the framework of their regional environmental, economic and socio-cultural setting, as well as overall development policies and plans, so that they are well related to the region.

Carefully planned and properly implemented integrated tourist resorts can bring substantial economic and social benefits, while also minimising those environmental, socio-economic and marketing problems often associated with uncontrolled tourism development.

An analysis of how some existing resorts have been planned, implemented and financed can yield valuable insights into the approaches, principles and techniques of resort development that have proven to be successful, as well as the types of problems that have been encountered. Although each country and resort area is unique, the experience gained from planning and developing different types of existing resorts can provide useful ideas that other countries may be able to adapt to their own needs, in their pursuit of effective tourism development.

This WTO study, which was conducted in 1990/91, analyses six resorts, all largely completed and representing various regions of the world and different types of development. For each case study, comprehensive details are provided on planning and implementation, including the current status of development. Economic, environmental and socio-cultural factors in planning and implementation are also analysed, as well as the development impact of these factors. The report evaluates the financing of both the infrastructure and superstructure of the resorts, the respective roles of the public and private sectors in financing, and financial policies and procedures applied. Finally, it assesses the potential of applying these planning and implementation procedures in other development projects around the world.

- **Nusa Dua Resort in Bali, Indonesia,** represents a medium-sized beach resort in an island environment that also offers outstanding cultural and scenic day tour attractions.

- **Pomun Lake Resort at Kyongju, Republic of Korea,** is a medium-sized inland resort based primarily on nearby historic and cultural attractions for day tours. It also offers its own diverse recreational facilities and activities.

- **Cancun Resort on the eastern Yucatan Coast of Mexico** is a large scale beach and marine oriented resort providing a wide variety of tourist facilities and activities, as well as comprising a related new town development.

- **Puerto Plata Resort in the Dominican Republic** is a medium-sized beach and marine resort that has served as a catalyst for regional tourism development.

- **The South Antalya Tourism Development Project** on the Mediterranean coast of Turkey is a prime example of a major beach tourism development planned in a large area of existing villages, agricultural land and a mountainous hinterland of parks and forests.
- **Lanzarote in the Canary Islands** is a case study of a controlled tourism development that was planned and implemented for a complete island destination reaching maturity.

The results of this study are designed to be used by national, regional and local government tourism policy makers and officials responsible for planning and implementing resort development, as well as by private sector enterprises and organisations involved in tourism development.

The study was carried out by two consultants, each visiting three of the resorts to observe actual development patterns. In addition to meeting with public agency officials and private sector organisations to obtain background information, the consultants also met with officials of the World Bank, International Finance Corporation and Inter-American Development Bank in Washington DC, to discuss their involvement in the different projects. Further information on the study may be obtained from the respective national tourism administrations (NTAs) of the countries in which the different resorts are located.

Chapter 2

NUSA DUA RESORT
BALI, INDONESIA

BACKGROUND

Tourism in Indonesia

Indonesia is the fifth largest country in the world, in terms of population, and encompasses some 13,000 islands, of which about 3,000 are inhabited. The country possesses a great diversity of languages, cultures, historic and cultural sites and natural environments which provide a wide range of attractions for international and domestic tourists.

Tourism developed more slowly in Indonesia than in some other Southeast Asian destinations during the 1970s for a number of reasons. These included its inadequate tourism infrastructure, facilities and services and the rather weak image of the country internationally. Because of the country's generally low income levels, domestic tourism was also limited. Since the late 1970s, tourism has expanded rapidly, from 501,430 arrivals in 1979 to 2.2 mn in 1990. Growth rates were particularly high during the second half of the 1980s. Domestic tourism has also grown in line with the country's economic growth and as a result of measures to encourage domestic travel by Indonesians.

Indonesia attracts a wide range of tourist markets. Of the 2.2 mn international arrivals to the country in 1990 — based on country of residence — 39 per cent were from other Southeast Asian (ASEAN) countries, particularly Singapore and Malaysia, and a further 23.5 per cent were from other parts of Asia, notably Japan, Taiwan, Hong Kong and the Republic of Korea. Europe generated some 22.2 per cent of arrivals, led by the Netherlands — because of historic links — the UK, Germany, France, Italy and Switzerland. North America accounted for 5.6 per cent, and 9.2 per cent were from Australia and New Zealand. Australia, in fact, was one of the earliest source markets for tourism in Bali. More than 75 per cent of all arrivals are holidaymakers, with the balance travelling on business and for other private reasons.

Seasonality is not especially marked, although the months of June to December attract the highest number of international visitors. Average length of stay is around twelve nights. According to a survey conducted in 1990, the average expenditure of foreign tourists in the country was US$1,197 for business travellers and US$967 for holidaymakers, with an overall average of US$967 1/. The highest spending markets were the Italians, Dutch and Japanese. In 1988, international tourist receipts totalled US$1,028 mn, representing 5.3 per cent of Indonesia's total exports.

The current medium-term national tourism development policy is focused on seven broad objectives: improved access to tourism areas; tourist promotion;

maintenance and improvement in the quality of the country's tourism product; application of an integrated approach to resort development; emphasis on marine and nature tourism development (without neglecting other forms of tourism); human resource development for tourism; and implementation of a tourism awareness programme for Indonesians. Pelita 5, the national development plan for 1989-1993, targets 2.5 mn - 3.5 mn international tourist arrivals a year by 1993.

Although Bali is the leading destination for leisure tourists to Indonesia, other regions of the country have also been, or are in the process of being developed. Some of these are beginning to attract significant numbers of tourists. The preparation of a national tourism development strategy is also currently underway.

Tourism in Bali

Bali is the best known of all Indonesian islands internationally, thanks to its rich Hindu culture of colourful ceremonies, variegated arts and crafts, temples, traditional villages and life styles, combined with its highly scenic natural environment of terraced rice fields, mountains, lakes and beaches. Tourism to the island did not really develop to any appreciable extent until the late 1960s and early 1970s. But it expanded rapidly in the second half of the 1970s and 1980s with the opening of several large hotels and a number of smaller, but often good quality hotels and guesthouses. As the accommodation supply increased, this stimulated the growth of small independent arts and handicraft shops, restaurants and other tourist-oriented enterprises throughout the popular tourist areas of the island. It is estimated that about 40-50 per cent of all international tourist arrivals in Indonesia visit Bali, either as their sole destination or as a stopover on multi-destination tours of the country. There are direct international flights to the island, accounting for about 22 per cent of total air passenger arrivals to Indonesia.

In the late 1960s, the government initiated an overall policy for tourism development in Indonesia, recognising that Bali was the logical place to focus their preliminary efforts. It was also recognised that since tourism in Bali had until then developed in an uncontrolled manner, it was essential to introduce some careful planning into future development. This subsequently resulted in the Nusa Dua resort project.

Current tourism development objectives for Bali, as laid down and approved by the provincial government, may be summarised as follows:

• To support and enhance the traditional religious and community customs of the Balinese society.

• To diversify the island's range of tourism facilities and to spread the benefits of tourism development to the various regions (of which four are identified for the island — East, West, North Central and South Central).

• To increase the social benefits of tourism through investments in education, manpower training and development programmes.

- To increase community benefits by targeting employment opportunities for locals and by promoting integrated community health and environmental management programmes.

- To incorporate measures, in the integrated programme approach, to ensure coastal protection and the avoidance of conflicts with areas designated for religious purposes.

- To increase the local inhabitants' awareness of these development objectives through public information programmes.

Evolution of the Nusa Dua Project

In 1970, an agreement was reached between the central government, the United Nations Development Programme (UNDP) as the financing agency, and the World Bank (International Bank for Reconstruction and Development - IBRD, and the International Development Association - IDA) as the executing agency, for the preparation of a regional tourism plan for the island of Bali. The plan, drawn up by French consultants, was completed and approved by the government in 1971 *(Figure 1)* 2/. It emphasised the need to concentrate on the development of international standard accommodation in an area where the potentially negative effects of tourism would be minimised and an adequate infrastructure could be provided, in other words, an integrated resort development. The plan identified the existing main tourism development areas of Sanur and Kuta and recommended the construction of a road network between the main attractions of the island, stopover points and the different resort centres. It was also recommended that development should be carried out in different stages.

The choice of site for the integrated resort was based on the following criteria, which were best met by Nusa Dua, located on the eastern side of the Bukit Peninsula:

- Accessibility from the international airport (Ngurah Rai), located on the isthmus between the capital city of Denpasar and the southern peninsula of Bukit.

- The availability of suitable land not already being used for irrigated rice cultivation or other high value agriculture.

- An attractive beach.

To help ensure the priority development of hotels in Nusa Dua, the government — after consultation with the World Bank in 1972 — limited the number of international standard hotel rooms outside the resort to 1,600 (including several hundred existing rooms) until 1985. This was the date when the Nusa Dua resort was initially expected to be operational. Implementation of the resort project was to be largely the responsibility of a newly-created, government owned tourism corporation, the Bali Tourism Development Corporation (BTDC). Infrastructure and common facilities of the project included water supply, sewage and solid waste disposal systems, electric power, telecommunications, internal streets and storm water drainage, landscaping and landscape irrigation, an 'amenity core' or resort centre, and a service centre. The resort was expected to attract private investors to build and manage the hotels and other commercial facilities in the resort. Several international advisers were to be attached to the BTDC.

Figure 1

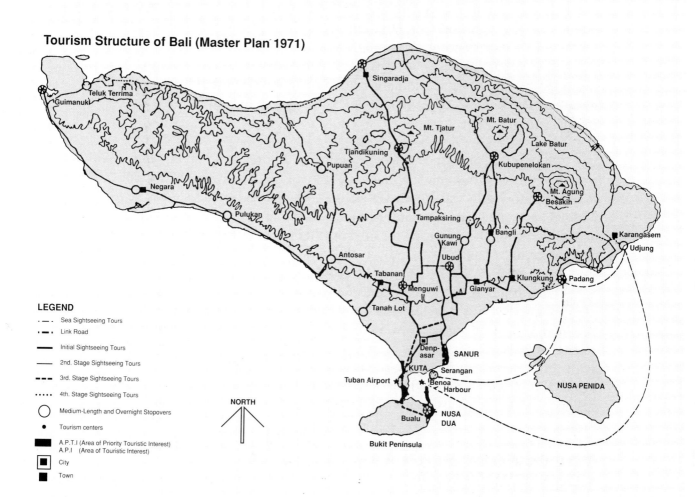

Tourism Structure of Bali (Master Plan 1971)

LEGEND
- · — · Sea Sightseeing Tours
- · ■ · Link Road
- ▬▬ Initial Sightseeing Tours
- ─── 2nd. Stage Sightseeing Tours
- ─ ─ ─ 3rd. Stage Sightseeing Tours
- · · · · 4th. Stage Sightseeing Tours
- ○ Medium-Length and Overnight Stopovers
- • Tourism centers
- ■ A.P.T.I (Area of Priority Touristic Interest)
  A.P.I (Area of Touristic Interest)
- ▣ City
- ■ Town

NORTH

Some infrastructure improvements were also planned for the two nearby villages of Bualu and Benoa, including the paving of roads, street lighting, public water supply and limited medical facilities. The project was to include construction of a new two-lane road between the airport and resort, connecting to a new road linking the resort and airport (and nearby Kuta tourism area) to the existing tourism area of Sanur and to the road network leading to the major attractions of south-central Bali and elsewhere. Some upgrading of existing road surfaces and replacement of inadequate bridges in the tourist excursion areas were also stipulated in the project.

The Bali Tourism Development Board (BTDB) was to be responsible for implementing the regional tourism plan, which required coordination between several government agencies, hotels and other private sector tourism enterprises, and Balinese community organisations. Technical assistance, in the form of various advisers, was provided to help the BTDB and government formulate and implement policies and programmes. These were designed to mitigate the potentially negative effects of tourism on Bali's social and cultural life, make the best possible use of the existing human and natural resources for tourism, and distribute the benefits of tourism in an equitable manner to the Balinese population.

The project included the construction of a hotel, tourism education and training centre — the financial responsibility of the government. A small demonstration farm was to be established to help local farmers grow vegetables and fruits suitable for sale to international hotels and restaurants. Technical assistance would be provided for improvements in the production and marketing of food items.

The project was budgeted at US$36.1 mn for the infrastructure and related components. Of this, US$18.1 mn would be required in foreign exchange. The IDA was to provide a credit of US$16.0 mn, covering 88 per cent of the foreign exchange required, or slightly more than 44 per cent of the total project cost, with the government financing the remainder. Some US$0.35 mn of the IDA credit was allocated for the retroactive financing of water investigations, well drilling and technical assistance to the BTDC.

THE RESORT PLAN AND REGIONAL CONSIDERATIONS

Resort Concept and Land Use Plan

A detailed resort plan was prepared in 1973 by a Japanese consulting firm. This was based on the conceptual land use plan for Nusa Dua incorporated in the 1971 Bali regional plan. 3/. This comprehensive study examined the regional planning framework and relationships and existing environmental conditions of the site. It made recommendations on the resort concept and specific land use, transportation, other components of the infrastructure, zoning regulations, site planning concepts, architectural and landscaping guidelines, renewal of the nearby villages of Bualu and Benoa, and implementation techniques and schedule.

The concept of the resort was that of an integrated high quality beach complex with self-contained recreation and commercial facilities. It was targeted at higher spending tourists in search of a high quality hotel and resort environment offering a wide range of facilities and services.

The plan, reproduced in *Figure 2,* shows the staged development of 2,500 hotel rooms in the first stage and 2,000 in the second stage in twelve beach-oriented hotel lots, with a centrally located amenity core (resort commercial centre) and festival park (cultural centre), and an auxiliary services area including a convention centre, traffic terminal and landscape plants' nursery. Other facilities included were a BTDC office, a service area for water and sewage treatment plants and sewage lagoons, open space preserved areas for parks on two offshore land-tied islets and along the shoreline, a sports park, an unspecified reserve, a boat jetty, and the internal road system including a roadway specially designed for a local shuttle bus service.

Figure 2

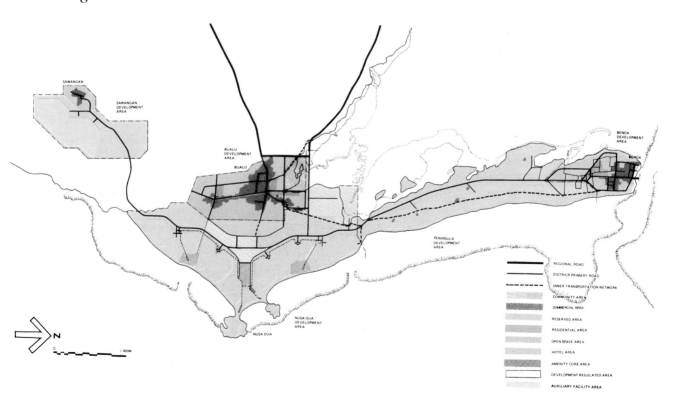

The land acquired for development was about 310 hectares. The site area is mostly flat with some hills inland where the golf course has been developed. There was little existing development on the site, except for coconut trees and a boat landing and storage area on the beach used by fishermen living in the nearby Bualu village. The plan also showed a possible third stage for development of hotels in an inland area near the resort and along the beach to Benoa village, but this was not part of the designated resort area.

Although the basic concept and layout of the plan were adopted and implemented, some minor changes were made during the course of implementation based on new circumstances. As an example, it was decided before development started to delete the two commercial sub-cores and to locate the National Tourism Education and Training Centre scheduled for Bali in one of the auxiliary facility areas. Somewhat later, it was decided to develop a 9-hole golf course in the unspecified reserve area and then a second 9-hole course extending into the auxiliary area and taking over one of the hotel lots.

More recently, about 400 condominium villas (duplex cottage units) associated with the golf course and 200 serviced apartments associated with existing hotels were added to the plan. The plant nursery proved to be uneconomic, as it was cheaper to purchase plants on the open market, so it was abandoned and the area was used for part of the golf course expansion. It was also decided that the Nusa Dua Beach pier, shown on the original plan, was unnecessary.

A revised plan was prepared in 1988 4/. This included recommendations for further improvements to the nearby villages, a bypass road system to serve these villages, and an implementation programme, as shown in *Figure 3*. The principal changes since this plan was prepared include the deletion of the proposed centrally located convention centre. Convention facilities were included in one of the resort hotels, and the originally designated area is being developed as part of the golf course expansion.

The resort plan included a number of development standards and design guidelines. A maximum building height of 15-m — applicable to all of Bali — was stipulated for Nusa Dua. This height limit was selected so that the top of buildings would be below the tops of the trees helping them to blend into the natural environment. Maximum density standards were established (the overall density of the resort is about 20 hotel rooms per hectare), with a maximum number of rooms set for each hotel lot. The maximum floor area ratio for each hotel lot was 0.5 and the maximum lot coverage by buildings was 25 per cent. It was stipulated that all utility lines were to be placed underground. A minimum 50-m distance from the shore-line was generally applied for main buildings, although a few recently developed hotels seem to have managed to get around that requirement.

Architectural design guidelines were established by a Design Review Committee. These were based on the use of traditional Balinese architectural motifs and some local building materials such as the distinctive Balinese style brick. Exterior advertising signs are strictly controlled with only directional signs allowed. As already mentioned, extensive landscaped park and open space areas were allocated in the plan. The preservation of the two islets as parks, integrated with a park area adjacent to the lagoon between the islets and with the shoreline landscaping and footpath, is worth special mention. Extensive landscaping has been integrated into the road network and existing trees on the site retained wherever possible.

Public access is legally required to all shoreline areas in Indonesia and this was applied in Nusa Dua, with access corridors provided from the central facility and internal transportation area to the beach. As recommended on the plan, one wide corridor has been developed to provide access for fishermen from Bualu to the beach where their boats are stored. The plan included the preservation of some small existing Hindu temples on the site. These are used by Balinese employees and are also of interest to tourists.

Resort Infrastructure and Employee Housing

The resort infrastructure was carefully planned and engineered to meet international standards and avoid any potential environmental problems. The internal road network, shown on the plan, was integrated with swale-type drainage-ways which are attractively landscaped and provide an open space feature. As mentioned, a separate road for shuttle bus service runs parallel to the major internal road that connects the hotels and other facility areas. As planned, the new two-lane road was constructed connecting the resort with the international airport, Kuta and Sanur, as well as the general road system that provides access to the major tourist attractions, such as artists' village, temples and scenic areas.

As development has progressed, the access point to the resort entrance — which is also the access to the Benoa Peninsula and village — has become congested. This is likely to grow worse with the continued development of the area. The 1988 plan proposed a by-pass road to provide a direct connection from the airport access road to the Benoa road, thus alleviating congestion at the resort entrance point. It also recommended a by-pass road around Bualu village to provide better access to that area. However, the main airport access road, which serves the villages as well as the resort, is also becoming congested and could get worse. So there is now talk of expanding this road to four lanes.

As far as the resort water supply is concerned, a well-field located several miles away from the resort was developed in the mid-1970s, with a pipeline extended to the resort service area where it was treated and distributed to the resort users. Separate potable and irrigation water distribution systems were also developed. Since the initial development, the resort's potable water system has been connected directly to the Denpasar water system, with the well-field water

Figure 3

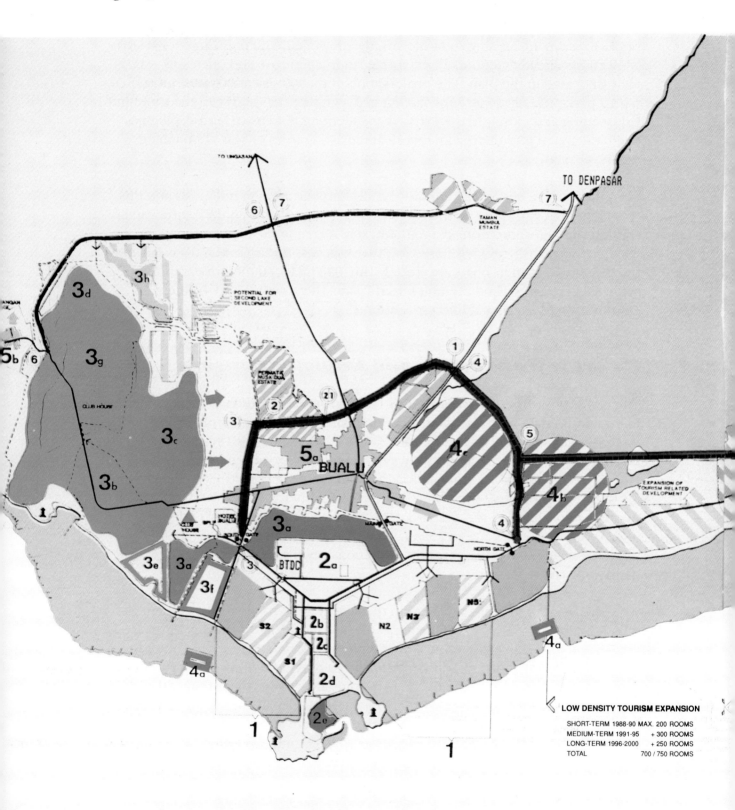

LOW DENSITY TOURISM EXPANSION

SHORT-TERM 1988-90 MAX.	200 ROOMS
MEDIUM-TERM 1991-95	+ 300 ROOMS
LONG-TERM 1996-2000	+ 250 ROOMS
TOTAL	700 / 750 ROOMS

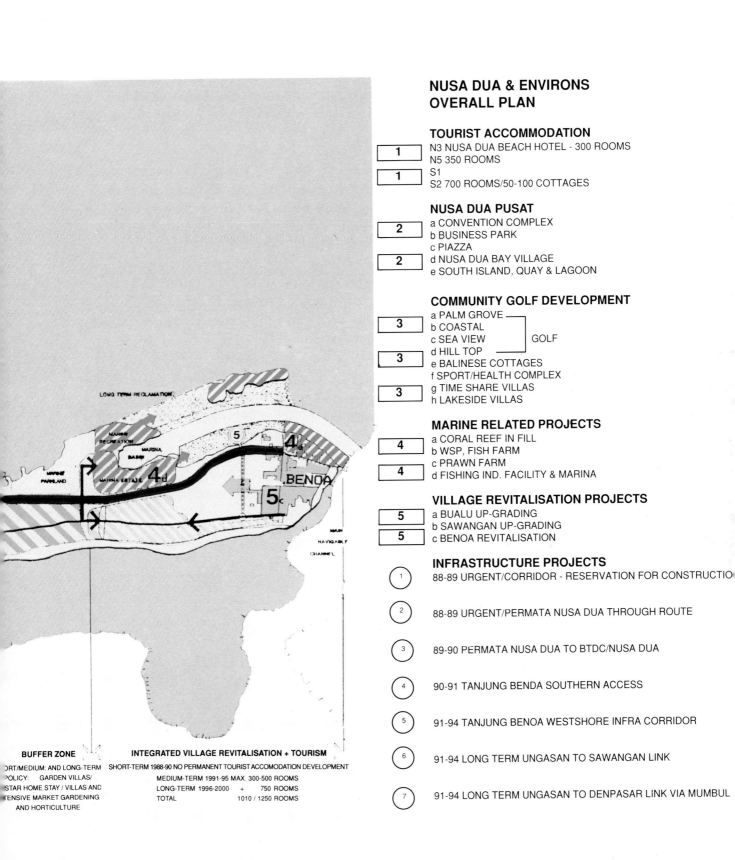

NUSA DUA & ENVIRONS
OVERALL PLAN

TOURIST ACCOMMODATION

1	N3 NUSA DUA BEACH HOTEL - 300 ROOMS
	N5 350 ROOMS
1	S1
	S2 700 ROOMS/50-100 COTTAGES

NUSA DUA PUSAT

2	a CONVENTION COMPLEX
	b BUSINESS PARK
	c PIAZZA
2	d NUSA DUA BAY VILLAGE
	e SOUTH ISLAND, QUAY & LAGOON

COMMUNITY GOLF DEVELOPMENT

3	a PALM GROVE
	b COASTAL
	c SEA VIEW GOLF
3	d HILL TOP
	e BALINESE COTTAGES
	f SPORT/HEALTH COMPLEX
3	g TIME SHARE VILLAS
	h LAKESIDE VILLAS

MARINE RELATED PROJECTS

4	a CORAL REEF IN FILL
	b WSP, FISH FARM
4	c PRAWN FARM
	d FISHING IND. FACILITY & MARINA

VILLAGE REVITALISATION PROJECTS

5	a BUALU UP-GRADING
	b SAWANGAN UP-GRADING
5	c BENOA REVITALISATION

INFRASTRUCTURE PROJECTS

- (1) 88-89 URGENT/CORRIDOR - RESERVATION FOR CONSTRUCTIO
- (2) 88-89 URGENT/PERMATA NUSA DUA THROUGH ROUTE
- (3) 89-90 PERMATA NUSA DUA TO BTDC/NUSA DUA
- (4) 90-91 TANJUNG BENDA SOUTHERN ACCESS
- (5) 91-94 TANJUNG BENOA WESTSHORE INFRA CORRIDOR
- (6) 91-94 LONG TERM UNGASAN TO SAWANGAN LINK
- (7) 91-94 LONG TERM UNGASAN TO DENPASAR LINK VIA MUMBUL

BUFFER ZONE
ORT/MEDIUM: AND LONG-TERM
POLICY: GARDEN VILLAS/
STAR HOME STAY / VILLAS AND
ENSIVE MARKET GARDENING
AND HORTICULTURE

INTEGRATED VILLAGE REVITALISATION + TOURISM
SHORT-TERM 1988-90 NO PERMANENT TOURIST ACCOMODATION DEVELOPMENT
MEDIUM-TERM 1991-95 MAX. 300-500 ROOMS
LONG-TERM 1996-2000 +   750 ROOMS
TOTAL   1010 / 1250 ROOMS

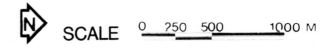

SCALE   0   250   500   1000 M

now being used in the resort irrigation system for use on the golf course and resort landscaping.

Electric power for the resort is provided directly from the island's electrical grid system as originally planned. The resort telecommunications' system is also connected to the general island system.

A separate sewage collection and treatment plant system was developed for the resort as there was no existing sewage system in this area. Sewage effluent is treated to a secondary level with the waste water, along with the well field water, supplying the resort irrigation system. Although consideration was initially given to the establishment of a solid waste collection and disposal system, the individual hotels decided that it was more economical to dispose of their solid waste by paying local companies to collect it. Part of it is then used in recycling operations such as for feeding livestock. This approach has not been totally satisfactory, however, because the waste material that is not reused is apparently often not disposed of elsewhere in a sanitary manner.

No housing for resort employees was developed directly on the resort, but land was made available adjacent to the access road and near the resort for private housing development. This has provided a total of about 800 units. One area was designated for higher quality housing and another for less expensive accommodation. Development of these areas is currently underway in line with demand. Some employees also live in the nearby villages and a large number live in Denpasar and elsewhere. Minibus service is available for employees commuting from these more distant locations.

Economic Impact Analysis

The World Bank analysis projected that the resort would provide direct employment for about 5,800-6,000 people in hotels and other establishments, with an additional 3,700 jobs generated for artists and handicraft workers, by 1983 — when it was originally expected to be fully operational. The economic rate of return was calculated at 18.7 per cent, with net foreign exchange earnings of US$8.5 mn in 1978 and US$36.2 mn annually from 1985 onwards. Central and local governments were also expected to receive substantial direct revenues from taxes generated by the resort operations. It is likely that these targets were achieved, albeit at a later date than originally planned.

Regional Relationships

As has already been explained, strong consideration was given in the resort planning to regional relationships. The resort site was selected and planned within the framework of the Bali regional plan, with the resort viewed as one important component of the island's overall tourism development structure. Regional road development was carried out as part of the project to provide good access between the resort and the airport and to other tourism areas and the island's tourist excursion road network. Much of the resort's other infrastructure was integrated into Bali's infrastructure systems.

The relationship of the resort development to the nearby villages of Bualu, adjacent to the resort and Benoa, about 3-km north of the resort, was considered especially important. In the past, these villages were isolated, highly traditional, had very limited infrastructure development and community services, and the villagers generally had low education, skills and incomes. One major objective was for the villagers to benefit from the resort development. The project incorporated plans to improve village roads, develop a village and rural water supply system from the resort system with public water taps provided, extend electric power to the villages and install street lighting. The provision of in-house water and electrical power supplies was an option, the cost of which was the responsibility of the individual householders. Some community services, such as the upgrading of medical clinics, were also financed by the resort developers.

Villagers were encouraged to develop small-scale enterprises such as handicraft shops and restaurants to serve tourists, and this has been very successful. The villagers also earn money from working in the resort and renting housing to resort employees and students of the Tourism Education and Training Centre. During the resort development, some villagers were able to work on construction projects and were given priority for this type of work depending on their skill levels. Young village locals were trained to work in the resort.

Despite the efforts directed at improving the nearby villages, it was recognised after the resort was opened that these villages required additional planning and encouragement for development. Thus, the 1988 plan includes sections on village upgrading plans and programmes.

DEVELOPMENT IMPLEMENTATION

Organisation and Responsibilities for Resort Implementation

As indicated in the initial agreement between the government and the World Bank, the Bali Tourism Development Corporation (BTDC) was established in November 1973 as a government-owned limited liability corporation to develop and manage the Nusa Dua resort project. The BTDC was responsible for developing the major infrastructure, including the internal roads, drainage, water supply and sewage disposal systems, common area landscaping and certain common-use facilities. The BTDC was also responsible for attracting hotel investment, negotiating with interested hotel management groups, and leasing hotel sites. As part of its promotional activities, the corporation prepared and distributed an investment booklet. The BTDC was also initially responsible for development of the amenity core and the leasing of commercial facilities in this centre. It established its main office within the Nusa Dua complex and a branch office in Jakarta.

Operation of the potable water supply system has since been transferred to the local government and, as was originally planned, the electrical and telecommunications' operations are integrated into the island-wide systems and run by the responsible agencies. Due to the difficulties in developing the amenity core, that project site has been leased to a private company for development and operation. The golf course development and operation, including a club house and sports centre, is contracted to a private company that will also be developing the condominium units referred to previously. The regional road improvements that were part of the project, but outside Nusa Dua, were developed by the country's highways' department.

Much of the technical work (planning, engineering, etc.) of the BTDC was contracted to consulting firms. Among the many technical advisers attached to the BTDC during its first years of operation were a development adviser, who assisted in promotional efforts to attract investors and carry out financial negotiations, engineering, architectural and agricultural advisers. Zoning regulations and architectural design guidelines were prepared for the resort development, based in large part on the recommendations of the 1973 resort plan.

The BTDC is currently organised under a Board of Supervisors or Directors and a managing director, with two directors — one for development and operations and the other for administration and finance. These two directors are responsible respectively for operations and development and finance and general administration, with various units and sections designated within these four divisions. In addition to the continuing development activities, the BTDC is now responsible for the following operational functions:

• Sewage collection and treatment.

• Irrigation system (supplied from the treated sewage effluent and the well-field).

• Common area landscaping and maintenance of the two islet parks.

• Maintenance of the internal road system.

• Operation of the internal shuttle bus service.

• Street lighting.

• Beach maintenance and security.

• Overall security of the resort's common areas.

• Fire protection for the resort.

• Emergency medical clinic (leased to the private sector).

• Hotel Bualu (a 50-room commercial hotel used as a training hotel by the Tourism Education and Training Centre).

In early 1991, the BTDC had 272 staff members including staff involved in security, maintenance and the Hotel Bualu. Based on its experience and success with the Nusa Dua resort, the BTDC is currently expanding its operations to develop new resorts elsewhere in the country. It is particularly involved in Manado in North Sulawesi and Biak in Irian Jaya, and has established some branch offices to develop those resorts. The BTDC is also planning other resorts elsewhere in the country. Although rather different from the Nusa Dua resort, they are being planned and developed as integrated complexes.

Resort Development Programming

Acquisition of land for the resort and infrastructure development was programmed and costed in detail by the World Bank, with a construction schedule incorporated into the 1973 Nusa Dua plan. The infrastructure was initially scheduled for completion by the end of 1976 and the resort scheduled to be fully operational by 1983. Land acquisition, which involved the purchase of private landholdings at market value, generally proceeded smoothly.

Since the land was relatively undeveloped, there was no issue about resettlement of existing residents. There were some, but not serious delays experienced in the development of the infrastructure, which was finally completed by the late 1970s. However, there was a major delay in attracting the first hotel investors, despite promotional efforts by the BTDC and investment incentives such as tax exemptions. Consequently, the first hotels were not opened until the mid-1980s. This initial difficulty in attracting investors was attributed by the government to the rather slow growth of tourism in Indonesia during the late 1970s and early 1980s and the restrictive air policy of that period, which limited the number of international airlines serving Bali. Another contributory factor may have been the usual reluctance of private investors to be pioneers in a new resort venture. Among the first investors were two government companies — PT Aerowisata, a subsidiary of the national airline (Garuda), and PTHI, a government owned hotel corporation. The development of Club Méditerranée in Nusa Dua in 1987 may have been helpful in demonstrating international investor confidence in the resort's viability.

With the opening of Indonesia to more international airlines, including increased direct flights to Bali, and the generally rapid growth of tourism to the country and Bali since the mid-1980s, hotel development in Nusa Dua has progressed rapidly and the resort is now virtually completed.

Regional Plan Implementation

The Bali Tourism Development Board (BTDB), with the governor as chairman and a technical staff including some international advisers, was also given responsibility from the outset for coordination of the Bali regional tourism plan. As an example, it carried out detailed land use plans for the Sanur and Kuta tourism areas, in order to improve existing development patterns and guide future growth, and plans for the first and some second stage tourist excursion roads identified in the 1971 regional tourism plan. The excursion road plans were aimed particularly at preserving fertile agricultural land, open space areas and scenic views adjacent to the roads, along which the linear development of arts and handicraft shops and tourist restaurants was beginning. It was proposed that instead of linear road development, a clustering of these commercial enterprises adjacent to existing villages should be encouraged. Implementation of these plans has been mixed, with some control exercised on excursion road development but apparently little implementation of the Sanur and Kuta plans.

The BTDB also coordinated aspects of the Nusa Dua resort development. Zoning regulations were written for the Nusa Dua resort and BTDB staff were involved in the Nusa Dua Design Review Committee activities. A multi-faceted socio-cultural programme was undertaken. For Nusa Dua, this was directed at monitoring the social impact of the construction phase of the resort on the nearby villagers, including educating the villagers about the project and how they could benefit from it. In other tourism areas in Bali, the BTDB conducted a public awareness programme. The BTDB also undertook surveys of tourist profiles and attitudes toward tourism development in Bali in order to provide a better basis for the effective planning, development and management of tourism. These activities have since been discontinued.

As mentioned previously, an agricultural development programme was attached to the Nusa Dua project with an agricultural adviser assigned to the programme for a few years. This programme was designed to help local farmers improve their production and marketing of fruits and vegetables for use in international hotels and restaurants. A small demonstration farm was established in Bali with some progress on the production of more suitable food. Although valid in concept, the programme was not highly successful overall, in part because the site selected for the demonstration farm was not as suitable as it might have been.

Education and Training of Resort Employees

One of the two national Tourism Education and Training Centres was located in Nusa Dua, as already mentioned, because of the close access to several major hotels. This centre, organised to serve several of the provinces of East Indonesia, was designed in an attractive Balinese architectural style and opened in the late 1970s. It was financed and is managed by the central government. The school initially received international technical and some financial (for equipment) assistance from the International Labour Organization (ILO). During its first years of operation, priority was given to Balinese who were to be trained to work in the Nusa Dua resort, but the school now receives students from all the various provinces.

Since the original local students had very limited general educational backgrounds, special remedial education programmes were organised for them by the school to bring them up to the entry acceptance requirements of the

18

school so that they could enroll in the regular tourism programmes. Many of the young villagers took advantage of this opportunity, completed their training programmes, and are currently working in the resort. Some of these have since taken the school's advanced programmes and have now been promoted to supervisory and assistant manager level positions in the resort hotels.

At the present time, the school offers a number of different certificate and diploma programmes — of up to two, three and even four years long — at the craft and supervisory levels in hotel and catering operations, tour and travel operations and tourism management, as well as short refresher and special courses for existing tourism employees. The school currently handles up to 2,000 students annually including short course participants. However, the school was designed to handle only 1,000 students and enrollment for regular students is therefore restricted. Since present capacity is limited, the government intends to relocate the school inland within the next year or so, and to lease the present site to an investor for resort purposes. It is expected that payment for this site will be sufficient to finance the new school development. All graduates of the school find employment, and there is considerable competition for places at the school, with about 3,000 applicants each year for the 250 regular programme entry places available. The development of the new school will enable twice as many students to enroll every year.

Current Status of Development

The Nusa Dua resort is nearing completion. As indicated, the land was all acquired during the early stage of the project, and both the internal and regional infrastructure, including access to the resort and in the nearby villages, was completed by the late 1970s. Since the mid-1980s, hotel development has progressed rapidly, as shown by Table 1.

All these hotels are of four or five star category. The convention centre, a separate complex on the Bali Indah Hotel site, contains a main hall with seating capacity for 1,800, a medium-size hall, an auditorium, 10 meeting rooms, a 1,000-seat capacity dining hall and exhibition galleries. The total 5,100 existing and planned hotel and other accommodation units exceeds the originally planned 4,500 units in the first and second stages of the resort plan. This is due to the addition of condominiums and serviced apartments. Consideration is being given to the development of another hotel but nothing is definite.

The first nine holes of the golf course are operational and the second nine holes were due to open in 1991. The golf club house is under construction. Development of the amenity core commenced in 1990. This will contain shops and offices as well as an amphitheatre for cultural performances, scheduled to be completed in mid-1991. As already mentioned, the Tourism Education and Training Centre was opened in the late 1970s, as was the BTDC office.

Table 1:
Current status of hotel development in Nusa Dua

Hotel	No. of rooms	Status
Existing Accommodation		
Hotel Club Bualu (training hotel & part of school complex)	50	Opened late 1970s
Nusa Dua Beach Hotel	450	Opened 1983
Melia Bali Sol	500	Opened 1985
Putri Bali	425	Opened 1985
Club Med Nusa Dua	400	350 rooms opened 1987; 50-room expansion planned
Nusa Indah Hotel & Convention Centre	360	Opened 1990
Bali Hilton Hotel	540	Opened 1990
Grand Hyatt Hotel Bali (on two hotel lots)	750	Opened 1991
Sheraton Lagoon Nusa Dua Beach	275	Opened in 1991
Total existing (on 9 lots)	3,750	
Planned Accommodation (as at 1991)		
Westin Hotel	350	Site lease signed
Pacific Island Club	400	Site lease signed
Condominium villas (by the golf course)	400	Planned
Serviced apartments (on existing hotels sites)	200	Planned
Total planned	1,350	
TOTAL ALL UNITS	5,100	

Some three and four star category beach hotels have been developed or are being planned outside the resort project area but along the adjacent Benoa Peninsula. These do not come under the BTDC, although they are generally compatible with the later stage recommendations of the 1973 plan. They are connected to the Denpasar water supply system in the same way as Nusa Dua. Discussions are also underway over the question of linking these hotels to the Nusa Dua sewerage system. Other hotels have been built, or are planned for the Jimbaran Beach area on the isthmus between the airport and Nusa Dua.

Socio-Economic and Environmental Impact

As far as the economic impact of the resort development is concerned, precise figures are not available. But it is likely that the projected generation of about 6,000 jobs is close to being achieved — based on an approximate 1.5 staff per hotel room, plus employees of the BTDC and golf course — and will be exceeded when the resort is fully completed. A significant, if unidentifiable number of jobs have also been created in the tourism supply sector for arts and crafts production and sales.

It is unclear how much foreign exchange earnings and government revenues in the form of taxes are generated by the resort, but estimates suggest projected targets will be met or even exceeded because of the high quality of development and related high tourist expenditure patterns.

Within the resort, there appears to be little negative environmental or socio-cultural impact because of the well developed infrastructure and strict land use and design controls applied. However, beach erosion is taking place adjacent to one of the hotels, and a retaining wall has been built to control further erosion. This problem is probably the result of natural coastal processes because there has been no disturbance of the Nusa Dua shoreline during the course of the resort's development.

It is unfortunate that the stretch of footpath in the common area along the beach by one of the developed hotel sites has been removed, thus interrupting the continuity of this pleasant public access way.

Some traffic congestion is being experienced on the access road, particularly near the resort entrance. It is expected that this will be mitigated once the new local bypass roads are developed and if the main access road is widened. The present system, whereby hotels operators are individually responsible for disposal of their waste to local entrepreneurs, may be generating some waste disposal problems outside the resort. In addition, since land use controls were not strictly applied to the areas along the access to Nusa Dua, there has been some linear commercial development with unattractive advertising signs, especially near the resort entrance.

The nearby villagers have benefited significantly from a socio-economic point of view as a result of the resort development, as was originally planned through the various programmes already detailed. As mentioned, plans have been prepared for further upgrading of the local village environment.

FINANCING OF PLANNING AND DEVELOPMENT

The original regional plan was financed by the UNDP and the central government. The financing of subsequent resort planning and infrastructure engineering was the responsibility of the BTDC. It was partly funded by a World Bank loan, although more recent resort planning has been financed from the BTDC's budget. The total infrastructure costs including the regional roads was about US$37 mn, or close to the original estimate. Of the proposed World Bank loan of US$16 mn, only US$14.3 mn was actually used. Of this, US$9 mn was used by the government to capitalise the BTDC and the remainder allocated to the highways department for regional road development. The balance of the financing was provided in local currency by the government through the BTDC.

Since 1987, the BTDC has been operating at a profit and, since 1989, has paid a dividend to the government as a shareholder, as well as paying corporate taxes. The agreement with the government is that the BTDC does not need to repay its initial capitalisation (including the World Bank loan to the government which is repaying the loan), but will instead pay dividends and corporate taxes. Some of the profits of the BTDC are being used to finance BTDC resort projects elsewhere, as previously described.

The primary source of revenue for the BTDC is from the leasing of hotel, amenity core, golf course and condominium development sites. The lease rent for the hotels is based on the allowable number of rooms for each site specified in the 1973 plan and is established as being equitable for both developers and the BTDC. Lease rents are set for a 30-year period with renegotiation for extensions at the end of that period. The cash flow of BTDC has been enhanced through the payment in advance of the total 30-year lease rent by two hotel developers. Other sources of revenue are user fees paid for the sewage service provided to the Hotel Club Bualu and other hotels.

Hotel financing was arranged by the respective investors involved and details have not been fully disclosed. As already stated, one hotel is owned by a government hotel corporation. The hotel financed and developed by PT Aerowisata has been sold to a joint venture company set up by an Indonesian group and the Sultan of Brunei. The Hilton hotel is totally owned by Indonesian interests. The other hotels are jointly owned by Indonesian and international companies. The BTDC has a small interest in one of the hotels, as well as owning the Hotel Club Bualu. The amenity core is leased to an Indonesian company and the golf course operation and future condominium development are joint ventures between Indonesian and international interests. There was no international agency financing involved in the development of hotels and other commercial facilities.

Various investment incentives including certain tax exemptions were and still are provided to the Nusa Dua investors and investors generally in Indonesia 5/.

Bali Hyatt, Nusa Dua
Resort

Local Balinese food on
display

Shoreline Park, Nusa
Dua, Indonesia

Nusa Dua footpath
linking the resort hotels

Local Balinese
dancing, Nusa Dua

Nusa Dua golf course

The extent of these incentives has been gradually decreased through the years as it has become easier to attract project investments.

OVERALL EVALUATION AND CONCLUSIONS

Resort and Regional Planning

The plan for the Nusa Dua resort has proved to be realistic and successful overall, providing a high quality, environmentally sensitive and functional resort that meets current market demands. The basic concept was maintained throughout its implementation despite some modifications.

It should be noted that, although the primary attractions of Bali are its rich cultural heritage and scenic beauty, past experience among tourists on the island has shown that most prefer to stay in beach accommodation, spending part of their time on sightseeing tours and the remainder, relaxing on the beach or around the hotel swimming pool and in recreational activities. This is the established pattern in the Sanur and Kuta resorts. Thus, the concept of developing a beach resort is valid even within the Bali context of cultural tourism. For tourists who wish to have more direct experience of village life, small scale accommodation and other tourist facilities are available in some of the Balinese towns.

With respect to regional relationships, the regional transportation infrastructure was suitably planned to provide access to the resort and from the resort to other parts of Bali, although it will require some further improvements in the near future to alleviate growing traffic congestion, especially near the resort entrance. In the nearby villages, proper consideration was given to both infrastructure improvements and programmes to provide socio-economic benefits to villagers. Plans are underway to further upgrade the environment of these villages.

Nusa Dua is seen by some observers as an exclusive resort designed only for certain high-spending market segments. However, it should be recognised that, within the regional context of Bali, Nusa Dua is only one development among a wide range of different types of tourist accommodation. Bali still caters to a diverse range of market segments. In fact, as has been mentioned, a number of three and four star hotels are now being developed quite close to Nusa Dua, thereby providing this immediate area with a greater variety of tourist facilities.

The resort was planned within the framework of a regional tourism plan for Bali which has proved in concept, to be an appropriate one. Detailed planning for other tourism areas was carried out as a result of this plan. With the development of Nusa Dua and the continued rapid growth of tourism in Bali, it is clear that the 1971 regional plan is now rather outdated and requires review and revision. In addition, the rapid growth of tourism has resulted in some development problems. Consequently, work on a new regional planning study has commenced, with assistance from UNDP. This will result in a comprehensive tourism development plan and the formulation of a tourism management programme for Bali.

The Nusa Dua project was the first integrated resort to be developed in Indonesia. Because of its environmental and financial success, it is seen as a model by the government and, as previously stated, the integrated resort concept has been adopted by the government for application in newly developing tourism regions elsewhere in the country.

Development Implementation

Despite the delays experienced in attracting hotel investment, the approach adopted for the Nusa Dua development seems to have been a valid one. The delay, it was recognised, was due largely to the inadequacy of international air access to the island; a more "open skies" policy has since been adopted. Modifications to the plans for implementation were relatively minor; contracting private companies for: the amenity core, golf course development and management and transfer of responsibility for a potable water supply to the Denpasar city water system.

The BTDC public corporation approach to the development of the infrastructure, and management and maintenance of the resort's common areas, roads and sewage system, with leasing of hotels and other commercial sites to the private sector has generally been successful. The BTDC has become a profitable venture and will probably continue to be viable. In addition to the facilities wholly owned by Indonesian private interests, the joint venture (international and Indonesian) approach to financing commercial development is consistent with overall national investment policy. Based on its experience with Nusa Dua and the financial resources available, not to mention the government policy of developing integrated resorts elsewhere in the country, the BTDC is now involved in developing resorts in other areas.

The planned regional road development and infrastructure improvements to nearby villages have been successfully completed, although it is recognised that road and village improvements must be continued. The social development and training programme has also been successful in generating socio-economic benefits for the villagers. However, the demonstration farm and agricultural programme — a concept from the original project — did not come up to expectations for various reasons.

The detailed planning for other tourism areas, prepared as part of the original project programme, was not satisfactorily implemented, either, except for some open space controls that were applied to the excursion roads. In fact, the relatively uncontrolled development of tourism, especially of small-scale enterprises, outside Nusa Dua is a cause of concern for the government and many residents. A new approach is required to ensure preservation of the distinctive environmental character of Bali, without discouraging local entrepreneurship.

Concern is also being expressed by Balinese about the perceived, and perhaps actual, loss of control over ownership of and employment in tourism enterprises to Indonesians from other parts of the country. With its dynamic tourism sector, Bali is attracting a lot of investment and an influx of Indonesians. It is hoped that the recently launched regional tourism planning and management project will address these fundamental issues and generate some positive proposals for the future development of tourism on the island.

Notes:

1. Biro Pusat Statistik (Jakarta).Pengeluaran dan Pandangan Wisatawan Mancanegara -1990.

2. SCETO. Bali Tourism Study. 1971.

3. Pacific Consultants, K.K. The Nusa Dua Area Development Plan. September 1973.

4. JCP, Inc. and PT Gitarencana Multiplan. Nusa Dua Area Tourism
   Development - Feasibility Study of Phase II Development. May 1988. This report was preceded by the report: JCP, Inc. in association with JTB (Japan Travel Bureau). Updating the Nusa Dua Area Tourism Development Plan. January 1987.

5. Indonesian Government Investment Coordinating Board. Indonesia - Brief Guide for Investors. April 1989.

Chapter 3

POMUN LAKE RESORT
KYONGJU, REPUBLIC OF KOREA

BACKGROUND

Tourism in Korea

The Republic of Korea offers a wide range of attractions linked to both its distinctive culture and history and its natural environment of scenic mountains, lakes and beaches. During the past two decades, international tourism has developed rapidly, with foreign visitor arrivals growing from 232,795 in 1971 to close to 3 mn in 1990 1/. In addition, domestic tourism has become important, reflecting the country's rapid economic development during the past several years, with increased disposable incomes and holiday time available to Koreans for vacations. Korea's well developed transportation system and the relatively short distances between urban and tourist areas facilitates travel within the country by both domestic and international tourists.

Of the total international arrivals in 1990, 55 per cent were from Japan — due to the proximity of the market and its historic links with Korea — and a further 15 per cent were from other Asian countries, particularly Taiwan and Hong Kong. North America, especially the USA, generated an 11.6 per cent share and Europe, 5 per cent. Some 12.5 per cent were overseas Koreans (living mainly in Japan and the USA) visiting their friends and relatives (VFR). According to purpose of visit in 1990, 58.4 per cent were on holiday, 13 per cent travelling on business, 11.6 per cent on VFR, and the balance for other private reasons.

The peak season for international tourism is May to October, although seasonality is not strongly marked. The average length of stay of international tourists was 5.5 nights in 1990. About one third of tourists came on group tours and the rest were FITs (fully independent travellers). The vast majority of tourists to Korea arrive at Kimp'o international airport in Seoul, making that city the primary tourist gateway to the country. Average visitor expenditure per trip in 1989 was US$1,304 2/. Although some 1.5 mn Koreans travelled overseas in 1990, there was (and has always been) a positive balance on the country's tourism account, with international tourist receipts (US$3.5 bn) exceeding expenditure on travel abroad (US$3.1 bn). In 1989, the country had 335 registered hotels with 37,148 rooms.

Government policy is for the continued development of both international and domestic tourism, and this sector has been given a relatively high priority in national development planning.

Tourism in the Kyongju Area

The Pomun (previously spelt Bomun) Lake Resort is located near the city of Kyongju, 400-km southeast of Seoul. Access from Seoul is by frequent express train or bus (about four hours' travel time), or by scheduled air service from Seoul to either Pusan or Pohang, with completion of the journey by road. The national high-speed highway (expressway) network connects Kyongju to other urban centres in the country. The Kyongju area offers perhaps the best known and most interesting historic sites in Korea. Kyongju was the capital of the Silla (also spelled Shilla) Kingdom (57 BC to 935 AD), and numerous kings' tombs (large circular mounds), Buddhist temples, a famous religious grotto and other religious and historic sites remain from that period. Tumuli Park, for example, contains more than 20 of these tombs and much of the historic area is designated as Kyongju National Park. Because of the outdoor nature of these sites, Kyongju has been termed an open-air museum.

The tombs have been well preserved, and two of the excavated tombs have been developed with small interior museums. The temples, grotto and other religious and historic sites have been well maintained or restored, and the Buddhist sites attract many domestic and international pilgrims as well as general interest tourists. The well developed Kyongju National Museum has a large number of Silla Kingdom artifacts as exhibits. A Silla Cultural Festival is held every year in October. The distinctive Silla style pottery is being authentically reproduced and is an important example of handicrafts on sale to tourists. The modern city of Kyongju, with about 150,000 inhabitants, is also an attraction for tourists who want to observe the bustle of a contemporary Korean provincial city. *Figure 4* is a tourist map of the Kyongju region, indicating the relationship of Pomun Lake Resort to the city of Kyongju and nearby site attractions.

Figure 4   **KYŎNGJU TOURIST MAP**

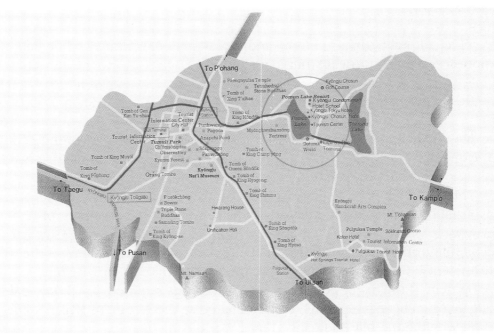

Before the Pomun Lake Resort was developed, the Kyongju area attracted some domestic tourists, including pilgrims, but relatively few international visitors because of the lack of suitable accommodation and other tourist facilities. Since the resort's development, Kyongju has become one of the major tourist destinations in the country and tourism is still expanding rapidly in the region.

Evolution of the Pomun Lake Project

In 1970, the government of the Republic of Korea expressed an interest in obtaining financial assistance from the World Bank (IBRD) for tourism infrastructure development in Korea. Following site visits by the World Bank team, the Kyongju area was selected for priority development (with Cheju Island as the second choice). In the course of project identification in 1972 and 1973, agreement was reached that the focus of tourist supply development would be on a new resort at Pomun Lake.

During this period, planning was carried for the Kyongju region according to the President's Instruction of June 12,1971, which stated: "Kyongju shall be rehabilitated so as to preserve and nurture the prominent natural scenic beauty, to revive the atmosphere of magnificence, brilliance, exquisiteness, magnanimity, progressiveness, composure, elegance and profundity of the ancient capital of the Silla Dynasty, thereby developing Kyongju as an international cultural and tourist centre".

The Tourism Development Planning Group was given the task of preparing a Kyongju regional plan for a ten-year period from 1972 to 1981 with the following major objectives 3/:

• Reconstruct the ancient capital of Silla with special emphasis on the recovery and revival of its original atmosphere ..., in accordance with the President's instructions.

• Preserve cultural heritage, enforce and spread national culture, refine national emotion and finally, provide tourist resources.

• Create an international cultural and tourist centre.

• Develop related industries, thereby enhancing the income level of the people of Kyongju.

This plan included the improvement of historic sites, tourist facilities, transportation such as roads, railroads and airports, the improvement of riverways, reforestation, agricultural development, water supply and sewage, telecommunications, electrical power, a city park and "readjustment of the environment". The plan also designated the Pomun Lake Resort site for development of the major portion of tourist facilities required. Total regional public investment requirements were estimated at US$72 mn, of which some portion would hopefully be financed by a World Bank loan.

According to the World Bank appraisal, the Pomun Lake Resort would be developed in its first stage for 3,000 hotel rooms on a site of 1,040 hectares. The project would include the provision of water, sewage and solid waste systems for the resort and city of Kyongju, construction of a multi-purpose dam (Duckdong Dam) and a small irrigation system, provision of electricity and telecommunications facilities, resort roads and street lighting, site preparation and common area landscaping, public facilities at the resort including a tourism centre, an amenity core with shopping and restaurant facilities, a small marina, golf course and community facilities, construction and/or realignment of access roads to historic sites, and the provision of training facilities for hotel and restaurant employees.

For water supply and sewage, the programme recommended the expansion of the Kyongju city water system to serve the resort and the development of a sewage and solid waste system serving both the city and resort. There would also be improvements made to the rural water supply, environmental sanitation, electricity and streets for five existing villages in the area, plus the development of an elementary school to serve these villages. The multi-purpose dam would be constructed upstream from the existing Pomun Lake (which was created by a dam constructed in 1921) to control flooding, stabilise the water level in Pomun Lake and supply water for the project area, the City of Kyongju and the villages, and facilitate a small agricultural irrigation project.

The Bank's total estimated cost for the project's infrastructure was US$50 mn, with a foreign exchange content of US$21 mn, or 42 per cent of the total. Proposed Bank financing was for US$25 mn which would cover the foreign exchange cost and provide US$4 mn for local cost financing. The remaining costs would be financed from the government budget. It was expected that private investors would finance and construct the hotels and a certain number of other tourist facilities. In addition to the immediate project cost, the government financed the historic site preservation, the Kyongju National Museum and other tourist attractions in the region, as well as regional infrastructure like the airports' and national expressway network that serves Kyongju.

It was agreed that responsibility for developing the project would rest with five government agencies. The Agricultural Development Corporation (ADC) would build the Duckdong Dam and related irrigation works. The Kyongju City Government (KCG) would be responsible for construction of the water supply and sewage and solid waste disposal systems of both the city itself and the resort. The Korean Electric Company (KECO) would construct and operate the electricity facilities of the project. The Ministry of Communications (MC) would install and operate the telecommunications' facilities. The Kyongju Development Office (KDO) would be responsible for implementation of all the remaining infrastructure works included in the project.

After construction, the KCG would operate and maintain the dam, the water supply, sewage and solid waste disposal systems, and all the project roads. The ADC and the Farmers Land Improvement Association (FLIA), or another suitable organisation, would operate and maintain the irrigation works. A new

Figure 5

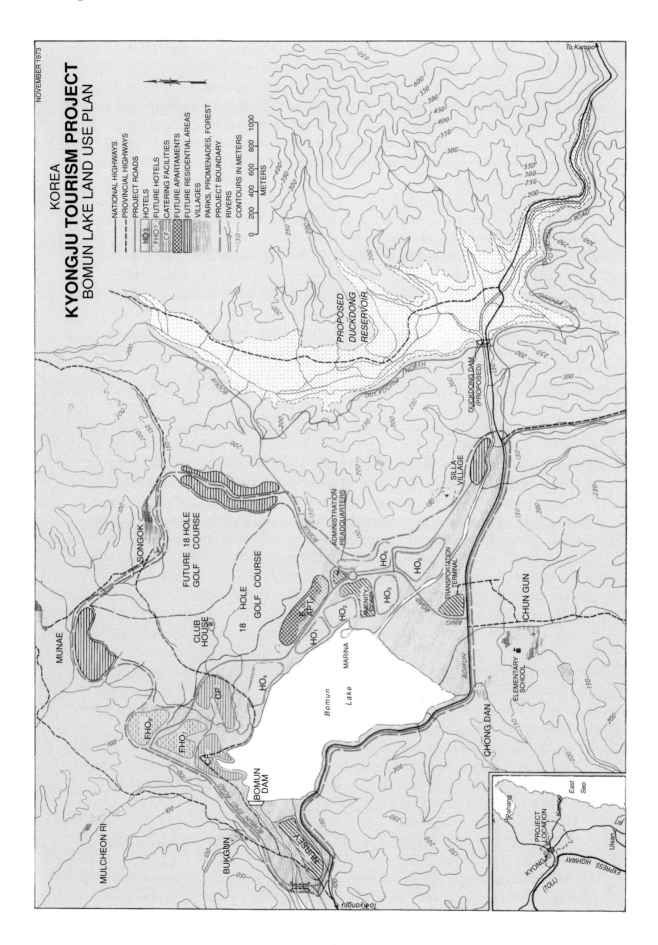

KOREA
KYONGJU TOURISM PROJECT
BOMUN LAKE LAND USE PLAN

NOVEMBER 1973

NATIONAL HIGHWAYS
PROVINCIAL HIGHWAYS
PROJECT ROADS
HOTELS
FUTURE HOTELS
CATERING FACILITIES
FUTURE APARTMENTS
FUTURE RESIDENTIAL AREAS
VILLAGES
PARKS, PROMENADES, FOREST
PROJECT BOUNDARY
RIVERS
CONTOURS IN METERS

METERS

0   200   400   600   800   1000

Figure 6

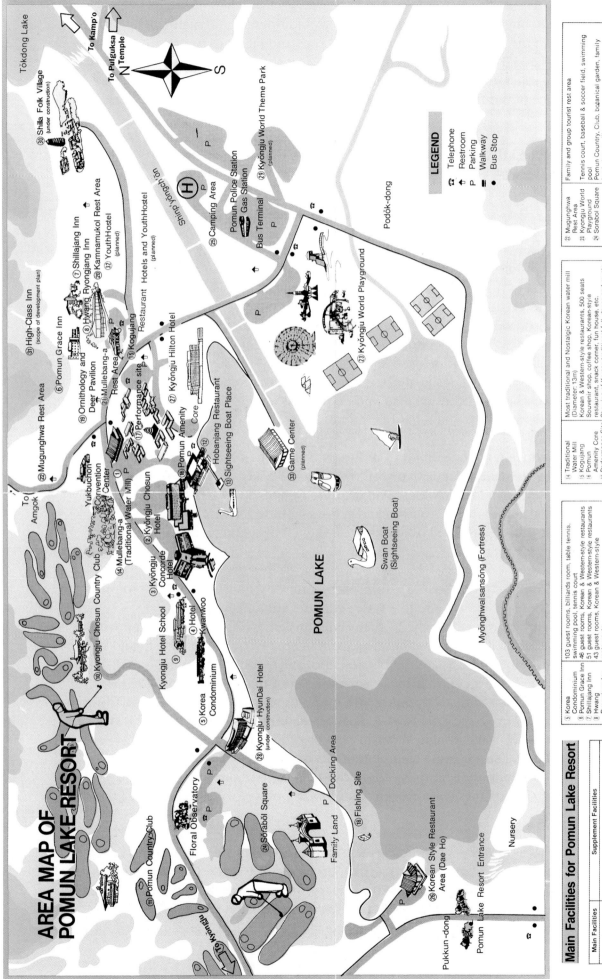

AREA MAP OF POMUN LAKE-RESORT

LEGEND

- ☎ Telephone
- 🚹 Restroom
- P Parking
- ● Walkway
- ● Bus Stop

Main Facilities for Pomun Lake Resort

Main Facilities	Supplement Facilities
① Yukbuchon	Int'l conference hall (900) seats showing of historical site film, tourist information center, post office, telephone, exhibition hall, etc.
② Kyongju Chosun Hotel	300 guest rooms, sauna, barber shop, beauty parlor, night club, swimming pool, tennis court, Korean
③ Kyongju Concorde Hotel	303 guest rooms, sauna, barber shop, beauty parlor, discotheque, swimming pool, tennis court, and Korean, Western & Japanese-style restaurants
④ Hotel Kwanwoo	50 guest rooms, coffee shop, sauna, banquet hall, Korean & Western-style restaurants
⑤ Korea Condominium	103 guest rooms, billiards room, table tennis, swimming pool, tennis court
⑥ Pomun Grace Inn	46 guest rooms, Korean & Western-style restaurants
⑦ Shillajang Inn	51 guest rooms, Korean & Western-style restaurants
⑧ Hwang Ryongjang Inn	43 guest rooms, Korean & Western-style restaurants
⑨ Kyongju Hotel School	Training institute for supplying qualified employees to Korea's Hotels
⑩ Chosun Country Club	36 holes, membership golf course
⑪ Pomun Country Club	18 holes, non-membership golf course
⑫ Hobanjang Restaurant	Korean-style restaurant, showing of traditional Korean dances
⑬ Sightseeing Boat Place	Sightseeing boat (Paekjohoi), yachting, boating

⑭ Traditional Water Mill	Most traditional and Nostalgic Korean water mill (Diameter: 13m)
⑮ Kogujang	Korean & Western-style restaurants, 500 seats
⑯ Pomun Amenity Core	Souvenir shop, coffee shop, snack corner, fun house, etc.
⑰ Performance Site	Showing of Korean traditional folk dance and music More than 20 sites, rental equipment available (Apr.-Nov.)
⑱ Fishing Site	
⑲ Ornithology and Deer Pavilion	Precious birds and deer ground
⑳ Kamnamukol Rest Area	Family and group tourist rest area
㉑ Mullebang-a (Water Mill) Rest Area	Family and group tourist rest area

㉒ Mugunghwa Rest Area	Family and group tourist rest area
㉓ Kyongju World Playground	Tennis court, baseball & soccer field, swimming pool
㉔ Sorabol Square	Pomun Country. Club, botanical garden, family land, deer pavilion
㉕ Camping Area	Water, supply shower, restroom etc.
㉖ Dae Ho	Traditional Korean-style restaurant
㉗ Kyongju Hilton Hotel	324 guest rooms, Sonje Contemporary Art Museum, banquet hall, health club, squash court, etc.
㉘ Kyongju Hyundai Hotel	Under construction

Scope of Development Plan

㉙ Kyongju World Theme Park	㉛ High-class Inn	㉝ Game Center
㉚ Shilla Folk Village	㉜ Youth-hostel	

Tŏkdong Lake

To Kamp'o

To Pulguksa / Temple

N S

㉚ Shilla Folk Village (under construction)

㉛ High-Class Inn (scope of development plan)

⑥ Pomun Grace Inn

⑦ Shillajang Inn

⑧ Hwang Ryongjang Inn

⑳ Kamnamukol Rest Area

㉜ YouthHostel (planned)

Restaurant Hotels and YouthHostel (planned)

Shiryoryong'ŏn

⑲ Ornithology and Deer Pavilion

㉑ Mullebang-a Rest Area

⑮ Kogujang

Koguyang

㉕ Camping Area

Pomun Police Station

Gas Station

Bus Terminal

㉙ Kyŏngju World Theme Park (planned)

㉒ Mugunghwa Rest Area

H

㉗ Kyŏngju Hilton Hotel

⑯ Pomun Amenity Core

⑰ Performance site

Hobanjang Restaurant

⑬ Sightseeing Boat Place

Podŏk-dong

㉓ Kyŏngju World Playground

㉝ Game Center (planned)

Yukbuchon Convention Center

⑭ Mullebang-a (Traditional Water Mill)

② Kyŏngju Chosun Hotel

③ Kyŏngju Concorde Hotel

To Amgok

Kyongju Hotel School

④ Hotel Kwanwoo

⑤ Korea Condominium

㉘ Kyŏngju HyunDai Hotel (under construction)

POMUN LAKE

Swan Boat (Sightseeing Boat)

Myŏnghwalsansŏng (Fortress)

Floral Observatory

㉔ Sŏrabŏl Square

Docking Area

⑱ Fishing Site

Family Land

㉖ Korean Style Restaurant Area (Dae Ho)

Pomun Lake Resort Entrance

Nursery

Pukkun-dong

Kyŏngju

⑪ Pomun Country Club

entity, the Kyongju Tourism Agency (KTA), would operate and maintain all public areas within the resort and lease and/or sell sites and facilities to private investors. The KTA was to be established not later than January 1, 1975. Overall project coordination would be provided by the Secretariat for Economic Affairs in the Office of the President of the Republic.

THE RESORT PLAN AND REGIONAL CONSIDERATIONS

Resort Concept and Land Use Plan

Following the World Bank appraisal and conceptual plan, detailed planning for the resort was prepared in 1973. This called for eight hotel sites and 4,000 rooms 4/. A revision to that plan was made in 1974, recommending that two of the proposed hotel sites be used for additional golf course development and reducing the number of rooms to 3,000. The present plan is still for 3,000 rooms. To reflect the increasing number of domestic tourists visiting this area, 1,000 rooms have been allocated for Korean style accommodation with lower tariffs and the remaining 2,000 rooms designated for hotels of international standard. *Figure 5* shows the original conceptual plan and *Figure 6* is a pictorial map illustrating the present plan, much of which has been developed.

The concept of the Pomun Lake Resort is that of an integrated, relatively self-contained, medium density resort providing a variety of accommodation, recreation and ancillary facilities. The resort is designed to cater to both international and domestic tourists and serve as a base for exploration of the nearby historic, cultural and religious sites, as well providing its own recreation and commercial facilities.

The land use plan shows six hotel sites, four of which are oriented to the lakeshore and lake views, one to a water channel and one, a hillside accommodation area where the Korean style inns are being developed and youth hostels are planned. A condominium apartment area is located on the inland side of the main resort road, as are the hotel school and associated training hotel. The resort is focused on a centrally located amenity core that includes an integrated shopping complex with an amphitheatre for cultural performances, an aquarium, convention centre, large Korean style restaurant and small marina on the lake front, post office, the Kyongju Tourism Agency office, and other community facilities. Fishing and boating facilities and activities are available on the lake. A pagoda structure in the shopping complex and a large traditional water mill wheel near the amenity core provide visual focal points for the central area of the resort.

The 18-hole and 36-hole golf courses are situated in the northern part of the resort. Also in the northern area is a small themed family park. On a lakeshore site south of the hotels is Doturak World Playground, an amusement park offering a variety of rides and recreation facilities, and an expansion area for the development of a theme park. A replica of a Silla style folk village is planned for a site near the Korean inns. There is a petrol station and bus terminal on the main access road.

Specific land use controls, development and design standards were prepared and applied to the resort 5/. These include procedures for submission' and approval of plans, general land use, architectural and landscaping standards and additional requirements for specific use areas. These standards function as zoning regulations for the resort, with each type of land use having its particular development standards.

Major hotels, for example, have a maximum allowable height of 45-m (12-15 stories), maximum site coverage by buildings of 20 per cent, and minimum setback from the lake shoreline of 10-m (although this setback is actually 12-14-m for the existing hotels). Outdoor advertising signs are prohibited and only identification, legal and construction signs are allowed. Exterior lighting is also controlled.

Architectural design must include consideration of climatic conditions, traditional architectural principles such as the Korean courtyard layout, and specific characteristics of the site location. Overall site planning must give attention to maintaining view corridors. No reflecting finishes on exterior walls are permitted except for glass and hardware items and exterior colours of buildings must be predominantly subtle and 'warm'. Landscaping principles to be followed are also specified. All utility lines must be placed underground.

The resort site of more than 1,000 hectares is flat near the lake shore and hilly further inland. This site was barren and undeveloped at the time of its acquisition for the resort development.

Infrastructure and Employee Housing

All infrastructure was developed to international standards. Water supply is provided by the Kyongju City system, which was upgraded as part of the resort project, and receives its source of water from Toktong Lake, created by Duckdong Dam as part of the project. In addition, this lake provides irrigation water for the resort. Pomun Lake is used for recreational purposes and provides some water supply for industrial purposes. Sewage collection and disposal are also provided by the city, whose sewage system was developed as part of the resort project. The sewage treatment plant is located about 10-km from the resort. Electric power and telecommunications are provided by the public utility agencies for the region. Solid waste collection and disposal are provided by the city of Kyongju, with some segregation and recycling of material, and the remainder incinerated if possible or disposed of in sanitary land fill. A storm water drainage system was part of the resort infrastructure plan and designed for the northern side of Pomun Lake where the resort facilities are located. This system involved a checkdam and sand basin to prevent sand flow into the lake and a total of 11-km of drainageways.

As originally planned, the regional infrastructure includes access to the resort, improvements made to some roads linking with historic sites, and some infrastructure improvements to five nearby villages, such as the development of an elementary school, as well as improvements to the Kyongju city water supply and sewage disposal systems.

No specific area was designated for major employee housing, but individual hotels provide some dormitory facilities for lower level employees, while many other employees find their own housing outside the resort, mostly in Kyongju. The hotels provide bus service for employees living in Kyongju.

Economic Impact Analysis

The World Bank appraisal included an economic analysis of the resort which indicated that, when fully operational with 3,000 rooms, the resort would provide employment for 5,400 people in the hotels and 1,500 employees in the other resort facilities. Indirect employment generated outside the resort could amount to 10,000-15,000 jobs. The economic rate of return of the resort development was estimated at 18.5 per cent. Net foreign exchange earnings generated by the resort were projected at US$66.4 mn per year from 1984 onwards, once the resort was fully operational. Economic analyses conducted in other reports in the early 1970s suggested slightly different figures, but still within the range of economic viability. A report prepared in 1980 analysed the financial situation of the resort up to that time 6/.

Regional Relationships

As has already been stated, much attention was devoted to planning regional integration of the resort. The resort, in turn, depends on the regional historical, cultural and religious sites for its primary support. The resort development was viewed as only part — although its role was seen as a major one — of the overall development planning of the Kyongju region. In addition to the regional attractions, the city of Kyongju was intended to be the 'service town' for the resort, providing much of the infrastructure and community services as well as housing and services for the resort employees. Some regional infrastructure improvements (water supply and sewerage systems) were included for the city as well as for the nearby villages; some road improvements were made to attraction sites. In addition to infrastructure improvements to the nearby villages, the application of zoning regulations to these villages was considered necessary in the plan, to control expansion of the villages. The plan also included statements that these villagers could obtain employment in the resort in the lower skilled types of jobs.

In addition to the project designated regional improvements, the government made major investments in preserving tourist attractions and developing visitor facilities related to these sites, and in the development of the Kyongju National Museum. As mentioned, some of the sites are in the Kyongju National Park . This reflects the fact that Kyongju is viewed as one of the most important historic places in the country, and should be conserved as a major element of the national cultural heritage as well as to attract tourists to Kyongju. The national highway network development also provided good access to Kyongju by routing an expressway from Seoul to Pusan through Kyongju.

DEVELOPMENT IMPLEMENTATION

Organisation and Responsibilities for Resort and Regional Plan Implementation

The Kyongju Development Office, an extension office of the Ministry of Construction, was established for the purpose of implementing the physical development of the immediate resort area development, and the Kyongju Tourism Agency was set up to develop and manage the resort. The various agencies' involvement in the major project components was as follows:

• Agricultural Development Corporation (ADC): To construct and equip Duckdong Dam with spillway and reservoir outlet works to Pomun Lake; construct and equip an irrigation system at the Bulguk area with reservoir outlet works, canals, flumes, conduits, tunnels and a pumping station; and land consolidation work at the Bulguk area.

• Kyongju City Government (KCG): To construct and provide expansion of the water supply for the City of Kyongju with a new water pump station and other improvements; install a new water treatment plant for the city; construct and equip a sewage system for the city with a sewage collection network and treatment system; construct and equip Pomun Lake resort with a water supply system, including a water treatment plant and intake at Duckdong Lake; install a sewage system for the resort; provide trucks for the collection of solid waste in the city and the resort; and provide water supply systems and environmental sanitation for the five nearby villages.

• Korean Electric Company (KECO): Construct and install an electrical supply system for the resort, with undergrounding of lines, and to the five nearby villages.

• Kyongju Development Office (KDO) and Kyongju Tourism Agency (KTA): The provision of a tourism infrastructure and facilities in the resort and nearby villages, including a storm water drainage network, environmental sanitation of the lake basin, earthworks and waterworks along the Shin Pyong River (in the resort area), the amenity and service core, an 18-hole golf course and club house, landscaping of the resort common area, and facilities in the nearby villages; construction of a street network of about 12-km within the resort area and the street lighting system; construction and equipping of a hotel school with facilities for about 250-300 students and a 30-room training hotel (expanded from 30 to 50 rooms in 1990); construction of four roads (including bridges) to provide access to historic monuments and scenic sites; construction of four roads (including bridges) to provide access to the resort; and relocation of three roads that would be affected by the Duckdong Reservoir development.

- Ministry of Communications (MOC): Construction and equipping of telecommunications facilities for the resort comprising telephone, telegraph, telex and fax, and subscribers' trunk dialling facilities.

In addition, the Ministry of Culture is responsible for conservation and maintenance of the various historic and cultural sites in the region.

The KTA was established in August 1975 by the Korean National Tourism Corporation (KNTC) to manage all aspects of the resort under the management of other agencies. The responsibilities of the KTA now include:

- Attracting private sector investment for commercial facilities and conducting negotiations with private investors.
- Management of the amenity core facilities, including the shopping complex and convention centre and several community facilities.

- Management and maintenance of common area landscaping and amenity facilities.

- Management of the 18-hole golf course and club house.

- Maintenance of the resort streets and street lighting.

- Tourist promotion.

The landscaping operations have proved to be quite successful and, based on its accumulated experience at Pomun Lake, the KTA is now providing landscaping services to other places in the country. With the development of Pomun Lake now scheduled to be virtually completed in the near future, the KTA has become involved in the planning and future development of a new marine resort at Kampo'o on the coast east of Kyongju. That resort will provide additional facilities for tourists and complement the attractions of the Kyongju area and Pomun Lake with marine recreation facilities. Kampo'o is also planned to include a golf course.

Throughout the development and management of the project, close coordination has been maintained between the major agencies involved. These are the Ministry of Transportation (which includes the Tourism Bureau), KNTC, KTA, the provincial government and Kyongju municipal government. The Tourism Bureau is responsible for the national level policy and planning of tourism and the KNTC is the tourism development and marketing arm of central government. The Pomun Lake Resort management agency of the KTA is organised into eight departments and 14 sections. In early 1991, it had a staff of 129.

Resort Development Programming

Development programming was specified in the 1973 Bomun Lake Tourism Development Plan. In agreement with the World Bank, the resort development was phased over the period 1973-82, when the infrastructure and 3,000 rooms were to be completed. The regional and resort area infrastructure development began in 1973 and was completed in 1979, much according to the original schedule, and the first two hotels were opened in 1979. However, there were some delays in attracting additional hotel investment until the late 1980s and the target of 3,000 rooms is now expected to be achieved by the early to mid-1990s when the resort is due for completion.

Education and Training of Resort Employees

The Kyongju Hotel School and associated training hotel, which also operates as a commercial hotel, have been operational for several years. The school offers a one-year programme in the various departments of hotel and catering and currently has about 270 students from all parts of the country. On-campus dormitories are provided for these students. The school offers modern training facilities, including equipment and classes in the application of computer technology in hotel operations. The school is under the general administration of the KNTC.

Current Status of Development

The total land area acquired for the resort development was 1,061 hectares with most of this purchased during the earlier stage of development. As previously indicated, the infrastructure was completed by 1979. The current status of development (1991) of accommodation and other facilities in the resort is shown in Table 2.

The KTA estimates that the resort will be about 90 per cent completed by 1992-1993, as is reflected in the above development schedule. The original level of 3,000 rooms, with about 2,000 of international standard (four and five star) and 1,000 of domestic standard (the Korean inns and youth hostels), is being generally maintained. In addition, a small number of hotel rooms are planned for development in conjunction with the public golf course club house. Outside the resort area, a few km away, two major hotels with full facilities (one contains a casino) have been developed.

Table 2:
Current status of hotel development at Pomun Lake

Type of Facility	Characteristics of Facility
Completed Facilities	
• Amenity Core	32 establishments of handicraft/ souvenir shops, snack bars, restaurants, duty-free shop, etc., aquarium, amphitheat repost office, water mill feature and other facilities.
• Convention Centre	Main hall of 900-seat capacity and other facilities located near the amenity core.
• Hobanjang Restaurant and marina	Korean style restaurant and small marina on the lakeshore near the amenity core.
• Kyongju Chosun Hotel	300 rooms, convention hall and other facilities (opened in 1979).
• Kyongju Concorde Hotel	303 rooms, convention hall and other facilities (opened in 1979).
• Kyongju Hilton Hotel	325 rooms and full facilities (opened in April 1991).
• Hotel Kwanwoo	50-room training hotel with facilities (opened 30 rooms in 1979 and 20 rooms in 1990).
• Korea Condominium	103 units individually owned and some of which are rented to tourists.
• 3 Korean style inns	Each with 50 rooms for total of 150 rooms.
• Doturak World Playground	Large amusement park.
• Pomun Country Club	18-hole public golf course and club house.
• Kyongju Chosun Country Club	36-hole membership golf course and club house.
• Kyongju Hotel School	Facilities for 250-300 students.
• Kogajang and Dae Ho	Korean style restaurants. restaurants
• Various tourist rest areas	Picnicking areas.
• Gas station and bus terminal	Located on resort access road.
Total accommodation rooms/ units completed by 1991	1,231
Facilities Under Construction and Planned	
• Kyongju Hyun Dai Hotel	437 rooms, under construction (scheduled to open in 1992).
• Kyongju Hilton Hotel	Planned expansion of about 375 rooms.
• New hotel	320 rooms scheduled to start construction in July 1991.
• Kyongju Chosun Hotel	Planned expansion of 60 family units.
• Korean style inns	Plans for 4 more inns of about 50 rooms each with a total of 200.
• Youth hostels	2 youth hostels with facilities equivalent to 500 rooms, scheduled to start construction in July 1991 andopen in 1993.
• Silla Folk Village	18-hectare replicated traditional village, started in 1989 and completion scheduled in 1993.
• Doturak World Theme Park	Planned as an addition to Doturak
• World Playground.	
Total planned accommodation rooms/units	1,892
TOTAL ACCOMMODATION UNITS	3,123

Panoramic view of Pomun Lake and resort facilities, South Korea

Two hundred thousand square meter Pomun Lake offers various water sports and recreational activies

A 14-meter high artificial waterfall situated within the recreational park

A traditional-style
Convention Center, the
largest of its kind in
Korea

As part the Pomun
Lake land-use plan, the
Pomun Country Club
includes a clubhouse
and a 36 hole golf
course

Pomun Outdoor
Theatre, which is in
front of the five-storey
Pomun Tower, offers
daily performances

Socio-Economic and Environmental Impact

Precise figures on employment generated by the resort are not available, but the KTA estimates that about 9,000 people will be employed in the resort when it is fully completed — somewhat higher than originally projected by the World Bank. It is likely that foreign exchange earnings will meet the projected target, based on the large number of international tourists visiting the Kyongju area and the resort. The financial viability of the KTA and existing hotels indicates that the originally estimated economic rate of return of the resort is being achieved.

The average annual room occupancy of the major hotels is about 70 per cent, with the peak seasons from April to June and September to November and the low seasons during the remaining summer and winter months. Some 60 per cent of guests are foreign tourists and 40 per cent are domestic visitors. Of the international tourists, the most important are Japanese (65 per cent share) and American. Although the hotels are financially viable, the resort management and hoteliers would like to reduce seasonality, and thereby increase the average annual occupancy rate. They plan to do this by developing more facilities and activities for winter season tourism. Discussions are currently underway on the subject of developing some existing hot springs at Pomun Lake with guest facilities for winter use. The average length of stay for both domestic and foreign tourists is a short two days and attempts are being made to increase this through the development of more activities, including the planned theme park and Silla Folk Village. The KTA also plans to offer daily cultural performances at the amenity core amphitheatre. Development of the beach resort at Kampo'o on the coast will provide more recreation facilities for the region.

Although the resort is financially viable overall, the shops in the amenity core are not doing particularly well and the KTA is offering them at low rents as incentives to potential shopkeepers. The family hill park development was apparently not financially viable and has been closed.

Within the resort area, there does not seem to be any negative environmental impact because of the well developed and maintained infrastructure and strict development controls applied to the resort. Only limited motor boating is allowed on the lake (most of the boats are non-motorised) and so there is little water pollution from boat motors.

Traditional Korean architectural styles have been applied to several of the facilities, especially to the amenity core, convention centre and independent restaurants. The club house of the 36-hole golf course is also attractively designed in the traditional style. This Korean styling of central facilities and, as mentioned, development of the traditional water mill with its large water wheel, gives the resort a distinctive character and sense of place. It should be noted that in Korea, as well as many other places in the world, it is more expensive to use and maintain traditional styles and materials than modern ones.

No negative socio-cultural impact of the resort was observed and the nearby villages have benefited from the infrastructure developed as part of the resort project and from employment generated by the resort.

FINANCING OF PLANNING AND DEVELOPMENT

Planning of the Kyongju region and Pomun Lake resort was financed by the Korean government, with some of the planning and special studies financed by the KDO and KTA using funds that included the World Bank loan for the project. The resort site land was mostly in private hands, although some areas owned by the government were transferred to the KNTC by the Ministry of Construction via the Ministry of the Treasury. Until 1985, the private landholdings were purchased by the KNTC based on the market value determined by a government appraisal agency. After 1985, land purchase prices were negotiated with the landowners. It was reported that there were some but no major problems in acquiring the land.

About one-half of the World Bank loan of about US$25 mn was used for the dam construction and related works, and the balance of US$12.8 mn was applied to other aspects of the resort development. The loan interest rate is 7.2 per cent. As of 1991, about one-half of this loan had been repaid.

Total KNTC and government capital (including the World Bank loan) invested in the resort and related infrastructure and facilities was about US$93 mn — higher than the originally estimated US$50 mn because of the additional facilities included and, presumably, an increase in costs. Total private investment, as of 1991, was estimated at US$186 mn.

The government investment included the infrastructure, amenity core and restaurant, KTA administration office, the convention centre, site land preparation, landscaping, street lighting, the 18-hole golf course and club house, tennis courts, hotel school and training hotel facilities, and rest area facilities for domestic tourists. Private sector investment has included the hotels and inns, condominium complex, 36-hole golf course and club house, the amusement park, family hill park, Silla Folk Village (under construction), petrol station, restaurants, and some other facilities. A privately developed game centre (casino) is planned for development but not yet implemented. The membership 36-hole golf course is operated by the Kyongju Chosun Hotel, and the Kyongju Concorde Hotel operates the small marina and associated lakeshore restaurant and will be developing and managing the Silla Folk Village (a US$5 mn project).

Resort sites for commercial use are sold to the private sector, with the price based on official appraisal of the market value of the sites. Incentives offered to attract private investment include exemption from certain regional taxes (registration, acquisition and property taxes) with the approval of central government, and provision for the purchase price of the land to be paid in installments over a 3-5 year period. In addition, low-interest, long-term development loans are available from the government as an investment incentive, and loans can be obtained from the government for up to 30 per cent of the total construction cost, with repayment of only the interest for the first two years and then the interest and principal during the next three years. Two of the existing hotels were originally constructed by the KNTC and later sold to the private sector. Private sector developments are mainly owned by Korean companies.

The KTA was initially capitalised by the KNTC. In addition to payments received from land sales, revenue sources of the KTA include:

- The public golf course operations.

- The 50-room training hotel which also functions as a commercial hotel.

- Landscaping business outside the resort.

- Shop rentals in the amenity core.

- Fees collected from the private sector enterprises for resort management.

The KTA operation is profitable. Following an agreement with the KNTC, the KTA does not pay dividends but is instead investing its profits in the new resort development at Kampo'o. It is reported that all the hotels are making a profit.

OVERALL EVALUATION AND CONCLUSIONS

Resort and Regional Planning

The resort plan, with its modifications, has proved to be successful in providing an attractive, environmentally sensitive and functional resort satisfying both international and domestic tourist markets. The concept of the original plan was valid and has been closely followed. Revisions to the plan were based on changing market needs. With the rapid economic development of the country and the increasing disposable incomes and leisure time of Koreans, it was recognised early in the development process that Korean style accommodation of inns and youth hostels and related leisure facilities were needed in the resort. Consequently, about one third of the accommodation units cater specifically to Koreans, with two thirds maintained at international standard levels, catering primarily to foreign tourists. This approach, including the development of the condominium units, has also contributed to giving the resort an interesting, diversified character attracting a variety of tourist markets.

Although the resort caters primarily to tourists who are visiting the historic, cultural and religious sites in the Kyongju region, it was realised that the resort also needed to provide a variety of recreational and other facilities. Since the principal tourist markets — Korea, Japan and America — to this area are golf-oriented, one of the originally planned 18-hole golf courses was expanded to a 36-hole course. Development of the amusement park and the proposed development of the theme park, Silla Folk Village and other facilities also reflect the approach of developing attractions and activity areas within the resort. The short average two-day length of stay in the resort hotels suggests that more could be done to persuade visitors to stay longer.

Thanks to the well developed infrastructure and the application of strict development and design controls, with provision of generous amounts of open space and landscaping, no appreciable environmental pollution has resulted from the project. The restrictions on motorised boats on Pomun Lake has controlled water, as well as noise pollution. The orientation of many of the tourist facilities to the lake shore and lake views has made the lake an important visual and activity feature of the resort. The use of traditional Korean architectural styles in the amenity core, convention centre and some other facilities, along with some special features such as the traditional mill with its large water wheel, has given the resort a distinctive environmental character.

The resort project planning included much consideration on the question of the regional integration of the resort. The resort is seen as one element of regional development and was planned within the framework of the Kyongju regional plan, with Kyongju viewed as the 'service town' for the resort. The infrastructure development was highly integrated regionally, with the major components of roads, water supply, sewage and solid waste disposal, electric power and telecommunications all developed as part of the national and regional infrastructure systems. In fact, the project included improvements to the Kyongju water supply and sewage systems, which benefited Kyongju city as well as the resort, and much of the World Bank loan and government contribution to the project was allocated to these regional improvements. Local villages near the resort were also upgraded as part of the project, as were some of the access roads to historic sites in the region.

Because the resort site was undeveloped when acquired, there was no social problem associated with relocation of existing residents. In addition, fertile land suitable for high value agriculture was not taken out of production for the resort development. The incorporation of infrastructure and community facility improvements to the nearby villages into the project has resulted in environmental and social benefits for the villages. The city of Kyongju has benefited environmentally through improvements made to its water supply system and the development of adequate sewage and solid waste disposal systems.

The direct and indirect employment generated by the resort has improved the socio-economic levels of regional residents, especially in Kyongju where many employees and their families live. Resort employment is expected to increase significantly in the near future once the new facility development is completed.

Conservation of the many historic, cultural and religious sites in the region has greatly helped preserve the cultural heritage of Korea, as well as providing major attractions for tourists. These sites are effectively presented to both Korean and international tourists through the development of visitor facilities and, more generally, through the excellent Kyongju National Museum.

Development Implementation

The organisational and financial approach to implementation of the resort development has been effective. The infrastructure was completed on schedule but, based on the original programme, there was some delay in construction of accommodation. However, according to the schedule of construction currently underway and commitments for future projects, the resort is expected to be about 90 per cent completed by 1992-93. The implementation approach originally proposed has been followed. Its effectiveness is due in large part to the close coordination maintained between the several different organisations involved in the development and between the public-type agencies and private sector companies. Although not part of the specific resort project, the role performed by the Ministry of Culture in conserving the historic, cultural and religious sites and developing visitor facilities has been significant. Efficient implementation of the hotel school project was an important factor in providing the trained employees essential for the type of service necessary in a high quality resort.

The basic organisational approach of the KNTC in establishing and financing the KTA, and the KTA's coordination of development of the infrastructure and central facilities and management of the resort has been an appropriate one for this resort. It should be noted that, in addition to hotels and other accommodation, many of the recreational and other tourist activity facilities of the resort have been delegated to the private sector for development and management. These include the 36-hole golf course, marina and lakeshore restaurant, the existing amusement park and proposed theme park and folk village. Only one of the smaller facilities of this type, the family park, was not financially viable, but its closure is reportedly temporary. Attracting private sector investment has been eased by the provision of various investment incentives from government.

The KTA is a profitable entity and it was reported that all the hotels are financially viable. Because of its experience at Pomun Lake and the financial resources available, the KTA is now planning to develop a new marine resort at Kampo'o on the nearby coast. The resort will be complementary to Pomun Lake, but offering a somewhat different type of resort environment and tourist activities. So it will contribute to the expansion of tourism in the Kyongju region, using the integrated resort concept and the established KTA organisational structure and experience gained from the Pomun Lake Resort project.

---

1. Ministry of Transportation and Korea National Tourism Corporation. *Korea — Monthly Statistics of Tourism.* 1990.

2. Ministry of Transportation and Korea National Tourism Corporation. *Korea — Annual Statistical Report on Tourism, 1989.* 1990.

3. Tourism Development Planning Group. *Kyongju Development Master Plan.* 1971.

4. Kyongju Development Office, The Ministry of Construction, Republic of Korea. *The Bomun Lake Tourism Development Plan - Physical Plan.* August 1973.

5. Kyongju Development Office, Ministry of Construction, Republic of Korea. *Attachment to Lease and Sales Agreement - Covenants and Restrictions Concerning Development Controls for the Bomun Lake Tourism Estate.* 1974.

6. Kyongju Tourism Agency and Arthur Young & Co. *Kyongju Tourism Project -Technical Cost Data, Tourism Statistics, Financial Information and Other Information.* March 1980.

Chapter 4

CANCUN RESORT
CANCUN, MEXICO

BACKGROUND

Tourism in Mexico

Mexico has had a long tradition of domestic tourism with beach resorts having been particularly popular with Mexicans during holiday seasons. The east coast port of Veracruz and the lakeside setting of Guadalajara were two early destinations for domestic tourists, partly because of their convenient access. Subsequently, the west coast town of Acapulco developed as a popular beach resort. As internal roads were improved and incomes increased, domestic tourism developed in a variety of other coastal areas, and it continues to be an important part of the Mexican life-style.

International tourism developed more slowly, but is growing increasingly important. There are three main types of international tourism in Mexico: urban tourism drawn to Mexico City, Guadalajara and other cities for business and cultural attractions; border tourism in the northern cities; and resort tourism. Urban and border tourism have expanded at a high rate in line with the growing economy of the country, but resort tourism was not as dependent upon the domestic economy and, therefore, took a different path of growth.

International resort tourism began to emerge in the late 1940s and early 1950s when Acapulco was discovered by tourists who were largely from the western USA. Resort tourism continued to expand, but not at the high rates of other competitive destinations like Hawaii and the Caribbean. The Mexican resorts that became popular with domestic tourists were also visited by international tourists, but problems of access and other secondary shortcomings impeded their development as international destinations.

In the late 1960s, the government prepared a National Tourism Plan and formed several institutions to assist with the development of tourism. The main objectives of this plan 1/ were to:

• Develop tourism in rural areas that have major tourist attractions and where alternative sources of employment are limited.

• Develop integrated tourist centres that stimulate regional economic development, not only in tourism, but also agriculture, industry and the arts and crafts.

• Improve and diversify the appeal of tourist attractions in Mexico.

44

• Generate increased foreign exchange through tourism, especially in the short term, since tourism has the potential, which other sectors do not have, to yield almost immediate returns.

The new institutions formulated a major long-term programme to develop five major resort areas throughout the country: Cancun, Ixtapa-Zihuatenejo, Loreto, Huatulco and Los Cabos 2/. The development of these planned beach resorts, including Cancun, encouraged a surge in resort tourism in Mexico. By the end of 1989, as much as 39 per cent of the total hotel room capacity in Mexican beach resorts was in these five planned resorts, and this share continues to increase as the resorts are further developed.

The number of international tourists visiting Mexico grew from about 1.3 mn in 1970 to 6.3 mn in 1989. The share of tourists arriving by air increased from 39 per cent in 1970 to 61 per cent in 1989, due largely to the growth of beach tourism as well as improvements in air transportation. The largest foreign source market continues to be the USA, although its share declined from 93.4 per cent in 1970 to 87.3 per cent in 1989.

This growth in tourism has generated substantial economic benefits. Income from tourism increased from US$415 mn in 1970 to more than US$2,980 mn in 1989, representing compound annual growth of 10.9 per cent over this period. Tourism was responsible for 2.8 per cent of the country's gross national product (GNP) and 14.1 per cent of foreign exchange earnings in 1989. There were an estimated 1.3 mn employees engaged in tourism activities and 144,127 hotel rooms in Mexico at the end of 1989. More than 45 per cent of these rooms were in beach resorts.

Tourism in the Yucatan Region

The Yucatan Peninsula is located on the east coast of Mexico, west of Cuba and Jamaica in the Caribbean. It was a centre of the ancient Mayan civilisation and many significant and visually impressive archaeological monuments remain in the region. Much of the present population of the Yucatan is descended from the Mayan people. The regional economy during most of the 20th century has largely been based on subsistence agriculture. The one agricultural crop that was exported, sisal, began to lose its market share to synthetic fibres in the 1960s. Today, the Yucatan Peninsula comprises three Mexican states, including the eastern coastal state of Quintana Roo in which Cancun is located. (see *Figure 7*).

While other Caribbean destinations had sizeable tourism sectors, only 60,000 tourists visited the Yucatan Peninsula in 1969, mainly to see the major Mayan ruins at Uxmal and Chichen Itza. There were only 100 hotel rooms on the mainland of Quintana Roo, another 300 on the large offshore island of Cozumel, and some 80 rooms on Isla Mujeres, a small island near the present Cancun.

The development of Cancun, which commenced in the early 1970s, greatly accelerated the expansion of tourism in the region. Once established, tourism

45

boomed not only in Cancun, but also in Cozumel and elsewhere along the Caribbean coast. The main tourist attractions of this region are the beaches and tropical climate, although the Mayan ruins continue to be of interest to visitors and the reefs near Cozumel attract a large number of divers. The number of hotel rooms in the region has steadily increased over the past decade, and occupancy rates have generally improved. One major interruption in this steady pattern of growth was caused by Hurricane Gilbert, which wreaked damage throughout the Caribbean in September 1988. Many coastal hotels in the region required some repairs but most were back in operation within three months. Nevertheless, the residual market impact of the hurricane carried over into 1989, when hotel occupancies continued to be much lower than in previous years. There was a strong rebound in tourist traffic in 1990.

Today, the Yucatan Peninsula is a major Caribbean tourist destination, and Cancun is the focus of tourism in the region. Cancun had 17,470 hotel rooms at the end of 1990, and registered 1.2 mn international and 395,200 domestic visitor arrivals that year.

Figure 7   **YUCATAN REGION**

The major tourist market for Cancun and the region is the USA, which accounted for a 57.6 per cent share of visitors to Cancun in 1990. The USA is followed by the domestic market which generated 24.9 per cent. Canadians and Europeans each accounted for 7.8 per cent. Average expenditure per foreign tourist in Cancun was US$576.

There is some seasonality in the Yucatan beach resorts. Hotel occupancies are generally over 75 per cent in the winter months from January to April and in July and August, while occupancies during the remaining months seldom fall below 60 per cent, except in September and October. The average length of stay in Cancun is around 5.2 nights, with foreign visitors generally staying 1.5 nights longer than domestic tourists.

Evolution of the Cancun Project

In the late 1960s, the Central Bank of Mexico was charged with conducting a comprehensive evaluation of the economy, including the tourism sector. It carried out a detailed two-year evaluation of tourism in Mexico and, in 1969, identified six (which later became five) tourism zones for development as described previously. In addition, the major implementing agency, Fondo Nacional de Infraestructura Turistica (INFRATUR), was formed in 1969 to implement the recommended tourism development.

Early in the evaluation process, the coastline of Quintana Roo was identified as a logical place for tourism development for a number of reasons. These included the geographic balance it would provide Mexican tourism, most of which was then located along the Pacific Coast. Five sites in Quintana Roo were considered. Several potential sites, including the islands of Cozumel and Isla Mujeres, were seen as unacceptable because of land ownership problems, while others were discarded because of a shortage of nearby water supply, access problems, few natural attractions, or other reasons. Cancun was selected as the best of the sites in late 1969.

The types of tourist markets destined for the Caribbean region were also seen as having great potential for Mexico, making Cancun the logical choice as one of the first five designated tourism zones in Mexico to be developed. INFRATUR, therefore, began to concentrate its efforts on Cancun, starting work on the master plan and beginning field surveys in 1970. The vast expanse of land required for the resort was purchased without great difficulty, since there were only 117 residents in the adjacent town of Puerto Juarez. Shortly afterwards, work began on an access road from Puerto Juarez as well as a temporary airstrip. At the same time, environmental studies were conducted of the large lagoon that is a main natural feature of Cancun. The studies provided methods to improve the circulation in the lagoon, and these were incorporated into the master plan.

When the master plan was completed, INFRATUR quickly commenced work on developing the infrastructure. At the same time, it was recognised that international funding could relieve the pressure that this project would place on national finances, which were already strained. Accordingly, application for financing was made to the Inter-American Development Bank (IDB), which issued a loan in 1971, mainly for the required infrastructure. With the loan in place, work proceeded rapidly on the airport, water supply, drainage, land reclamation, sewage system, and telecommunications. The airport was largely completed in 1974. The construction of several hotels began even prior to the completion of the infrastructure, all of which were financed with debt-equity from INFRATUR. In addition, an advertising and promotional campaign was launched in the international travel trade.

In 1974, the institutions responsible for the development of tourism in Cancun and elsewhere, including INFRATUR, were consolidated into a new organisation, Fondo Nacional de Fomento al Turismo (FONATUR).

The initial stage of development proceeded at a remarkable pace as much of the preliminary infrastructure was completed and three hotels opened in 1975. A year later, there were 2,023 rooms in Cancun, which supported an estimated workforce of 5,000 and a town of 18,000 inhabitants. FONATUR realised that this pace of growth would soon require additional infrastructure and a second credit facility was arranged with the IDB in 1976.

The first hotels were operating with good occupancy rates only a few years after opening, partly as a result of their popularity with domestic tourists. The average occupancy in Cancun rose from 68.6 per cent in 1977 to 70.9 per cent in 1978 and 77.5 per cent in 1979. These positive results in the early stages of development spurred the sales of hotel sites and the development of accommodation. The number of rooms increased to 5,258 and the population swelled to 70,000 in 1982.

Some problems caused by the unexpectedly rapid growth of the project surfaced in the early 1980s. Employees' housing supply was not keeping pace with demand and the disposal of sewage effluent was generating 'algae bloom' in a lagoon. Corrective measures were taken to mitigate these problems.

After 1982, approximately 400 hotel rooms were opened during each of the next several years, in spite of the weak financing market then prevailing in Mexico, which had encountered general problems associated with managing its large international debt. As a means of reducing this debt, the debt-equity swap was employed at Cancun. This approach resulted in a surge of new hotel development that began in the late 1980s and has only recently slackened. Today, there are about 18,000 rooms in more than 110 hotels in Cancun, and more hotels are being constructed in the tourism zone and in Cancun City, the residential zone of the project. The population is expanding too rapidly to allow for an accurate count but various sources indicate that it is likely to be near 300,000 (1991) and still growing.

THE RESORT PLAN AND REGIONAL CONSIDERATIONS

Resort Concept and Land Use Plan

The original concept of Cancun was that of a large, self-contained, integrated, modern beach resort with a total of some 30,000 hotel rooms, which has since been reduced to approximately 25,000 rooms. Most resort hotels would have beach frontage and most were to be built with at least a four star rating. The resort was designed to encompass 12,700 hectares. It was anticipated that the principal market would be foreign visitors from the USA, with a smaller segment comprising domestic tourists.

The geography of Cancun, with its long, thin band of land and beach enclosing a large lagoon is the most striking physical feature of the resort site. The beaches along the Caribbean shore are excellent and the mainland portion of the project was generally a dense scrub forest. There are underground streams of fresh water that flow into the lagoon system. The land use plan, presented in *Figure 8,* is largely determined by this distinct geography.

Figure 8

CANCUN RESORT PLAN

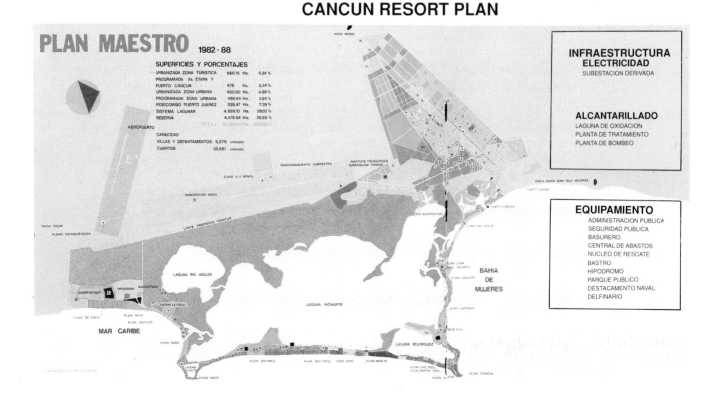

There are four main elements of the plan: the beach oriented hotels and related tourist facilities (tourism zone); the new town (urban zone); the international airport; and conservation areas. While the main commercial element of Cancun is the beach resort, a large expanse of land was provided to support the residential community — a complex that was to be built in conjunction with the resort. The international airport was planned at the southern end of the resort and large areas were reserved for conservation purposes. Less than 18 per cent of the area was in the tourism zones, another 29 per cent was in the urban zone, and the remaining 53 per cent, including the lagoons, was designated for conservation.

The tourism zone generally encompasses all the area along the stretch of land and beach between the lagoon and the sea, which is often referred to as Cancun Island, since it is separated from the mainland by two narrow channels spanned by bridges. The tourism zone was divided into three areas to correspond with the expected phasing of development. The first part comprises that portion of Cancun Island from the town to just beyond Punta Cancun, most of which lies perpendicular to the shore. The second extends along the strip lying parallel to the shore between a point near Punta Cancun and Punta Nizuc. This plan for staging was generally followed in the implementation process, although a revised plan in 1989 amended the land uses of the third stage by changing designated hotel uses to an amusement park.

The geography of Cancun allowed a large number of hotel sites to have a waterfront orientation but also promoted a linear configuration of development. To soften this pattern, development densities were varied somewhat along Cancun Island, with clusters of high density development interspersed among low and medium density areas.

A number of amenities were planned in the tourism zone including an 18-hole championship golf course, a large marina, several retail centres, a convention centre, piers, water sports facilities, and other recreation facility areas. Some existing Mayan ruins and other archaeological sites were preserved. A marine transportation system within the lagoon was designed but never fully implemented due to environmental considerations. In addition, several sites were reserved as public beaches for townspeople and day visitors.

Various design regulations were imposed on development in the tourism zone. These had several purposes including the provision of a high standard of lodging as well as an urban setting that would be in harmony with the environment. Four classifications of density were established: low, medium, medium-high, and high. Sites designated to be low density were limited to 75 rooms per hectare and a building height limit of three stories. High density sites would be allowed 150 rooms per hectare, 20-story buildings, and a lot coverage of 45 per cent. The bulk of hotel sites were assigned medium density zoning, which allowed buildings of five to eight stories. There are strict controls on advertising signs.

Some landfill operations were undertaken to widen narrow sections of the island, to stabilise the road providing access to the airport, to construct the golf course, and to enlarge a few hotel sites. The fill was provided by dredging both an adjacent bay and the lagoon. Dredging of the lagoon also had a salutary effect of improving its water circulation.

The new town, shown in *Figure 9*, is located at the northern end of the project and was designed to expand alongside the Merida-Puerto Juarez highway, which runs perpendicular to the coast. Progressive town planning principles were applied to the layout and land use composition of the support town. Development was planned to take place in separate 'superblocks' and provision was made for greenbelts, public beaches, educational, health, public safety and other community service functions, and commercial centres. The roadways were generally designed to include sidewalks and accommodate public transportation. Specific portions of the town were identified for development in each of the three stages of the overall resort development. The location of the international airport was selected for its isolation from the resort and town in order to limit the impact of noise and avoid land use conflicts.

Conservation zones, principally designed to protect the lagoons, were established in the initial plan. Subsequently, additional parcels of land inland from the lagoon, which were not owned by FONATUR but were under the jurisdiction of the Municipality of Puerto Juarez, were also designated for conservation. These additional parcels were to prevent development along the coastal federal highway and thereby limit the pollution of the underground fresh water streams that flow into the lagoons of Cancun. There are generous greenbelts along most of the interior roads in the project and sidewalks facilitate pedestrian traffic.

Figure 9   CANCUN CITY PLAN

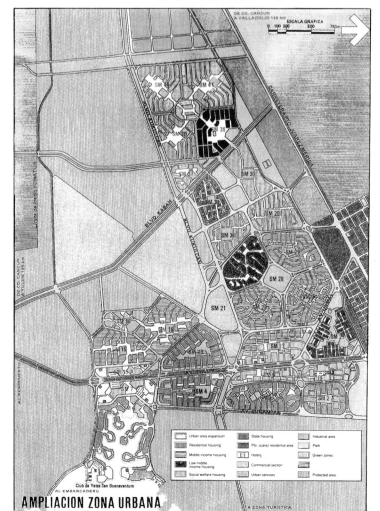

There is one major activity centre located near Punta Cancun. It encompasses the convention centre, the handicrafts centre, an indoor shopping mall, other retail complexes, and several restaurants. This centre attracts most Cancun visitors although it is far from many of the hotels that are situated at the southern end of the resort. The centre is rather sprawling, especially the retail shops, and has little architectural character. It would have benefited from more detailed planning with the application of design controls, based on a clear concept of its role in the overall project.

Ongoing planning continues to refine the resort development. Two major projects are currently proposed by FONATUR. One, Puerto Cancun, involves the development of an extensive European-style yacht marina and lodging complex which is designed to attract very affluent visitors. The second, San Buenaventura, is an upscale, largely residential waterfront development with plazas, promenades, and traditional architecture that would provide an interesting community environment with an historic character. In addition, the continuing expansion of Cancun City is being planned at the north of the resort in order to mitigate any environmental damage to the underground aquifer and the lagoon.

Infrastructure Considerations

The resort infrastructure was designed to international standards in order to fulfil the twin objectives of developing a complex which would be competitive with successful international resorts elsewhere and would be environmentally sensitive. It was also designed to allow phased construction and, in some cases, future expansion not specifically identified in the plan.

The airport, which was built with a runway of 2,700-m, was initially constructed to accommodate medium-sized jets. Provision was made for the future expansion of the airport to allow for wide-body aircraft. Sufficient land was allocated for the extension of the runway to 4,000-m. The initial terminal was small but also designed to allow for expansion.

The road system took account of the traffic that it expected to handle on completion of the resort. The principal arterial on Cancun Island is a divided four-lane road. This easily handles the current level of traffic which is rather low since few hotel guests use cars. Most guests use the frequent local buses within the resort and a high proportion of them take tour buses when travelling to the regional attractions. In addition, there is good van service from the airport to the hotels. The road system in Cancun City was also designed to handle greater levels of traffic than are now being generated and the superblocks were laid out to provide dispersed commercial centres to which many residents can walk. Most roadsides are planted with palms and other attractive landscaping.

One of the main attributes of the site was the fresh water available from the inland aquifer, located at 30-km from Cancun. The required wells, transmission lines, and storage facilities were initially built to serve a local population of about 30,000. The capacity of this system was subsequently increased.

The sewage system was designed for a secondary level of treatment, that is sufficient treatment for irrigation use. The initial design of the system provided for three treatment plants on Cancun Island and one oxidation pond facility in the new town of Cancun City. The effluent from the treatment plants was designed to be, and is currently, used for irrigation of the golf course and landscaped common areas.

The expansion of the resort generated an excess supply of nutrient-rich effluent which was then discharged into Laguna Bojorquez. The inadequate circulation in this lagoon contributed to the previously mentioned algae bloom and other environmental problems, including an unpleasant odour and unsightly clumps of algae. To correct this situation, injection wells were drilled near Punta Cancun and the excess effluent was discharged underground. But there are still a large number of homes in Cancun City that are not connected to the municipal sewage system.

The initial electric power supply was provided by transmission lines from the power plan in Merida (the main city of the Yucatan Peninsula), and subsequent additional power was provided through the national grid system. The telecommunications installation consisted of a 1,000-line system, which was regularly augmented as demand increased. An insect abatement programme was also undertaken to control mosquitos and other insects, principally through the use of insecticides.

Employee Community

As mentioned previously, the development of a new town for employees and their families was a major element of the plan. The planning, acquisition of land, and installation of the basic infrastructure of this town was the responsibility of FONATUR (then INFRATUR). The housing was to be developed largely through the existing programmes of various housing and financing agencies of the federal government.

The housing strategy faltered during the initial stage of development and for several years afterwards. Most of the migrating employees became squatters, moving onto neighbouring lands which were not owned by FONATUR. One reason for the problem was the rigidity of the loan mechanisms of the federal housing institutions, which made it difficult for many of the early employees of Cancun to obtain special low-income housing loans. Moreover, many of the migrating employees treated their employment as temporary. This was because they were unaware of, or unsure of, the long term prospects for employment and living conditions in Cancun City, or because they planned to eventually return to their homes. Within a few years after the opening of Cancun, settlements of squatters were mushrooming and the planned city had very little housing.

As Cancun matured, the illegal settlements began to take on some permanence. Street patterns emerged and illicit electric power was installed in the homes. It was apparent that many employees were no longer sceptical about staying in the region.

In 1981, the state government launched a multi-faceted housing programme which involved the sale of partially completed homes, loans for building materials, special low income loans, and other measures. In addition, FONATUR ceded approximately 800 hectares to the municipality for the development of additional housing. The temporary settlements eventually disappeared and were replaced by conventional housing. This major housing programme was effectively discontinued in 1987, having largely served its purpose.

The new town, now Cancun City, is a sizeable urban area with, as mentioned, a population of about 300,000. It is a modern city and seems to function well. A continuous issue being addressed by the community is that of the need for urban expansion, with as many as 100,000 new residents expected by 1995. The plans of the municipality are for the expansion of the town to take place mostly on lands lying north of the existing city, mainly to avoid environmental conflicts with the lagoons of Cancun. In addition, there will be a considerable amount of housing provided, albeit for more affluent residents, at the previously mentioned San Buenaventura project being sponsored by FONATUR.

Regional Relationships

The region of Cancun had a very limited economy prior to the development of the resort. The population of Quintana Roo was only 88,150 in 1970 and the territory had little cultivated land. The economy of the neighbouring state of Yucatan had been largely based on the agricultural crop of sisal which, as mentioned, had been displaced by synthetic fibres and was therefore being subsidised by the federal government.

The Cancun project greatly altered the economy and society of the region. Quintana Roo now supports a considerably larger population, with most of this growth attributable to immigration from not only other areas of the Yucatan Peninsula but also from other states throughout Mexico. Much of the population now resides in urban centres, whereas it had formerly been rural. Most of the regional planning that preceded these changes was conducted as part of the Cancun project — and that was limited — and there has been little subsequent regional planning.

The Cancun project promoted the development of regional infrastructure including the international airport, the regional highway system, water supply, electric power, and telecommunications. In addition, the conservation of Mayan archaeological sites has been accelerated as a result of tourism development. For example, the initial loan from IDB contained funds for the restoration and development of the ruins at Tulum, one of the attractions for Cancun tourists.

There has been additional tourism development in the region, especially on the island of Cozumel and along the southern coast of Quintana Roo. Cozumel, which accommodated 172,600 tourists in its 2,492 rooms in 1989, has become a major centre for diving tourism and also has a small international airport. The

Panoramic view of the
Cancun Resort area,
Cancun, Mexico

Cancun Resort area,
with its first stage of
development
completed

One of the many hotel
developments situated
within the resort area

Mayan ruins, located
near the tourist beach
area

Aerial view of the hotel
development along the
Cancun shoreline

Mayan ruins, one of
the most attractive
features of the Cancun
area

southern coast of Quintana Roo has several isolated beach areas on which some tourism projects have been built and more are planned. FONATUR's intention is to sponsor the development of luxury accommodation of a higher standard than in Cancun along the southern coasts and it is exercising its authority in the approval process to further this objective. While projects on the southern coast are proceeding, few are as successful as Cancun. Some of these resorts feature condominium projects and time-sharing programmes to enhance their early financial returns.

In addition to the archaeological sites, the region has extraordinary natural attractions and various conservation measures have been employed to protect the ecology in sensitive areas. The 1.3 mn acre Sian Ka'an Biosphere Reserve and World Heritage Site, located in the southern part of Quintana Roo, is a designated wilderness area with diverse ecosystems. In addition, a marine preserve with strict control measures has been established at Cozumel to protect the fragile reef ecosystem.

DEVELOPMENT IMPLEMENTATION

Implementing Organisation

The Central Bank of Mexico was an ideal organisation to assume the lead role in the development of tourism because it had considerable technical expertise, access to internal and external sources of funding, and was a technical and not political entity. The Central Bank prepared the initial supporting and policy development studies and then a quasi-subsidiary organisation, INFRATUR, was formed to implement the following principal objectives:

• Conceive and implement tourism infrastructure projects that complement investments of the federal government.

• Develop tourism infrastructure projects that generate private investment.

• Acquire, develop, sub-divide, sell and lease property associated with tourism projects.

• Collaborate with other government agencies in the promotion of tourism.

The founding trust agreement of INFRATUR provided for its termination after 30 years. INFRATUR subsequently merged with a fund created to finance tourism projects which evolved into FONATUR. The new functions of FONATUR included those of INFRATUR as well as financial activities in tourism, including the guaranteeing of loans, making temporary equity investments, trading loans and issuing credits.

While INFRATUR is actually a trust fund with its own resources, the Central Bank retains strong ties to FONATUR. For example, an arm of the Central Bank was the borrower on record for the two IDB loans, mainly because of its previous experience with international lending and its established credit resources. Furthermore, the Central Bank indirectly holds two of the six seats on the chief authority of FONATUR, the remainder being held by the Departments of the Presidency, Finance, Tourism, and National Patrimony. The financial management of FONATUR is under the Comptroller General.

FONATUR was responsible for the design and construction of all infrastructure and common facilities required for the Cancun project. It also was in charge of the promotion of the project and performed a variety of functions associated with the financing of many of the initial hotel developments. FONATUR contracted domestic consultants to perform various planning and engineering services. These supplemented the work of its own technical staff in the design and supervision of the construction of the infrastructure and resort facilities.

Most of the resort infrastructure was funded through FONATUR but the construction was typically the responsibility of the relevant public agencies such as the Department of Public Works or the Department of Water Resources. FONATUR was responsible for coordinating the work of these other agencies. On completion, the infrastructure was given to the appropriate utility or public authority which would then operate it and charge user fees. At times, the operation and maintenance of some of the infrastructure by the local public agencies has been deficient but on the whole, the operating standards have generally been satisfactory. FONATUR continues to maintain the common facilities and perform other functions in Cancun.

Resort Development Programming

Development schedules, detailed cost estimates and other elements of the programming of the Cancun project were prepared in the initial stages of the project. One key development schedule was prepared by INFRATUR in support of the application for the first IDB loan in 1971. This schedule estimated that the first hotels would open in 1973 and that there would be 1,140 rooms in Cancun in 1975 and 1,630 rooms open in 1980. In fact, the first hotel did not open until late 1974, but there were 1,322 rooms on line in 1975 and 3,930 rooms completed in 1980. Thus, the results exceeded the programmed schedule for 1980.

These forecasts were based on Cancun quickly penetrating the international travel market. Instead, foreign airlines were unwilling to incur the initial operating losses that were expected from operating scheduled flights to Cancun, and the international travel trade was reluctant to book hotel rooms in Cancun until the destination proved to be desirable. Fortunately, the appeal of Cancun to domestic tourists was much stronger than anticipated. While the initial share of the market contributed by domestic tourists was expected to be between 10-20 per cent, the actual share was 63 per cent in 1976 and more than 47 per cent in 1980. This domestic market support was instrumental in the development of Cancun.

The actual costs of the infrastructure turned out to be much higher than the original estimates. The cost overruns were attributed to the unexpectedly high inflation rate and the expanded scope of work in the dredging operations and the new town infrastructure.

As the project evolved, revised development schedules were prepared. Most of these schedules were very optimistic about the pace of development. Even though the development of Cancun proceeded rapidly, it often lagged behind the ambitious schedules.

Education and Training of Resort Employees

INFRATUR implemented an excellent training programme in construction skills during the initial stages of the project. The purpose of this programme was to provide agricultural workers, many of whom were Mayans, basic skills in the construction trades, thereby facilitating their employment in the construction activities of Cancun. The programme consisted of a two-month course in Spanish language training (many Mayans only speak their native language) and the use of construction tools and techniques. By 1976, more than 3,000 construction workers had received training through this programme.

In contrast, the programme established to train hotel employees was not considered to have functioned adequately throughout the 1970s, despite funding provided for this programme under the second IDB loan. A major reason was that tourism enterprises were in great need of employees and would hire and train most of those available even if they lacked sufficient skills. To remedy the shortcomings of the organised training programme, the Department of Tourism convened a meeting of local tourism and other government officials in Cancun in 1979 that identified problems and solutions. The hotel training programme was subsequently revitalised and its operations have improved. Today, this vocational programme, which offers three-year certificates to a few hundred graduates each year, is an integral part of the tourism sector. All graduates can find employment in Cancun.

Current Status of Development

The Cancun project has become a major international resort which currently contains 112 hotels and similar establishments providing approximately 18,000 rooms. The resort has a small convention centre, a championship golf course, retail centres, and a variety of water sports facilities. There is a wide variety of accommodation, with 72 mainly beachfront hotels on Cancun Island and another 30 commercial and budget accommodation facilities in Cancun City. This diversity allows Cancun to attract a wide variety of tourists.

Most of the hotels on Cancun Island were built to a very high standard. About 34 per cent of the rooms on Cancun are classified as Gran Turismo (six star), another 32 per cent are five star, and 18 are four star properties, according to the ratings of FONATUR in 1990. Moreover, the quality of newly opened and planned hotels is improving significantly. Excellent Marriott and Conrad (Hilton Corporation) hotels have recently opened, and two luxury projects (a Ritz-Carlton and a project of the Aoki Group of Japan) are planned.

Cancun suffered greatly from Hurricane Gilbert which damaged much of the landscaped areas of the resort. While the occupancies of the hotels improved greatly in 1990, room rates were still lower than expected. In the urban zone, there was rather serious damage to buildings, parks, and infrastructure, with public services adversely affected. The lower earnings from tourism since the hurricane have diminished the resources of both the hotel industry and public sector that are needed for the repair and maintenance of structures and landscaping.

As previously described, the new town of Cancun City has developed strongly, with the present population being about 300,000. This is expected to increase to 400,000-500,000 when the resort is completed.

The resort is not yet fully developed. The two large projects of San Buenaventura and Puerto Cancun, which will together require an investment in infrastructure of US$225 mn, are still in the planning stages. As mentioned, these projects are designed to be interesting activity-oriented and themed developments, attracting affluent tourists, and will further improve and diversify the resort. The continued development of the resort is projected to reach an inventory of over 25,000 rooms on completion, probably by the late 1990s.

Economic Impact

Economic considerations featured strongly in the conception and formulation of the Cancun project. As already indicated, the original objectives of the national tourism plan included the generation of employment in rural regions as well as foreign exchange earnings to improve the national balance of payments. The Cancun project, an outgrowth of the national plan, has been successful in satisfying both of these objectives.

The project analyses prepared by FONATUR, as well as those of the IDB, found the project to be economically viable. The detailed economic analysis prepared in conjunction with the IDB loan issued in 1971 produced the following estimates of tourism development and economic benefits in 1980:

Number of tourists	252,400
Hotel rooms required	1,630
Hotel employees required	2,710
Effect on balance of payments	US$25.8 mn

When this analysis was undertaken in 1971, the internal rate of return of the project was estimated to be 20 per cent, but all assumptions on which this estimate was based were exceeded. In fact, more than 460,000 tourists stayed in the 3,930 rooms in Cancun in 1980. Economic benefits generated by the expansion of development since 1980 would of, course, be much greater than those projections.

Today, the impact of Cancun on the economy of Mexico is significant. Total expenditure by foreign tourists arriving in Cancun by air was an estimated US$670 mn in 1990, which represented approximately 3 per cent of the foreign exchange earnings of Mexico and about 20 per cent of the total tourism earnings of the country. In addition, some of the domestic tourism generated by Cancun has undoubtedly diluted some foreign travel by Mexicans, thereby improving the overall balance of trade of the tourism sector.

The bulk of the economy of the state of Quintana Roo is derived from tourism. More than 20 per cent of the population of Quintana Roo lives in Cancun City, but Cancun was also the catalyst for tourism development in other areas of Quintana Roo and throughout the Yucatan Peninsula. The per capita income in the region is generally greater than in most other regions of Mexico due to the relatively higher earnings from tourism. However, the price of food in the region is reportedly the highest in Mexico because of the substantial demand generated by tourism enterprises and the high costs of transporting food to the Yucatan Peninsula.

Socio-cultural and Environmental Impact

The changes occurring in the region have been largely welcomed by the current residents, most of whom have moved there for employment and now have improved living conditions. The recent unemployment rate in Cancun has typically been very low, and incomes and education levels are much higher than in similar regions in Mexico. The original plan of Cancun City provided for extensive social services including police, fire, health, education and other government facilities. Due in part to this planning, the Cancun City community has functioned reasonably well but it is continuously being strained by the persistent growth of the city.

The impact of the Cancun project on the Mayan population in the region has generally been positive. The original programmes designed to facilitate the training of agricultural workers in the construction trade were apparently successful. Moreover, a study conducted in 1979 for the IDB found that a large number of Mayans had made the transition from agriculture to tourism and that Mayans participated in the various economic activities in proportions almost identical to those of all employees in Cancun 3/. Nevertheless, some tourism officials indicate that Mayans are often employed at low level jobs partially because of their difficulties with languages. Tourists receive some exposure to the Mayan culture in Cancun, but there appears to be greater opportunity for Mayan and Mexican cultural performances, exhibits of arts and crafts, and other cultural interchanges than is currently being realised.

The environmental impact of the Cancun project appears to be limited. No major artificial structures have been constructed on the beaches and some that were built, such as piers, were damaged by Hurricane Gilbert. Beaches were severely eroded in a few areas by Hurricane Gilbert but these are slowly being restored by natural accretion.

The most fragile ecosystem of the resort is that of the Cancun lagoons. The circulation in these lagoons was initially improved, substantial adjacent lands were designated for conservation, and boating activity has been restricted. As mentioned previously, one problem was the substantial amount of nutrient-rich effluent which was discharged into a small lagoon with poor circulation and then caused much algae growth. Subsequently, the effluent was instead injected into deep wells and other algae control measures were implemented. The Cancun lagoons are being carefully monitored by a number of environmental groups and it appears likely that the natural beauty and ecological functions of the lagoons will be retained.

FINANCING OF PLANNING AND DEVELOPMENT

The funding for all the planning of Cancun was provided by the Central Bank either directly or, after 1969, through its subsidiary, INFRATUR/FONATUR.

The infrastructure was initiated with funding from FONATUR and the largest portion of the subsequent financing was also provided by FONATUR, with some input from two IDB loans. FONATUR contributed more than 70 per cent of the total costs of the infrastructure work associated with the first IDB loan and over 60 per cent of that covered by the second loan facility.

The first loan, arranged in 1971, covered various infrastructure components necessary to support the initial hotel development, some improvements on Isla Mujeres, and the restoration of archaeological sites on the Yucatan Peninsula. The estimated cost of the work covered under this loan was US$47.1 mn, of which the IDB contributed US$21.5 mn, all in foreign exchange. When additional work was added and inflation increased, the total costs increased to US$73.2 mn, which was absorbed by FONATUR. The second loan, initially funded in 1976, provided for additional infrastructure in both the tourism and urban zones of Cancun, including construction of a secondary school and expansion of the hotel school. The estimated cost of the project was US$49.5 mn, of which US$20 mn was funded by an IDB loan.

An important source of income for FONATUR was the sale of hotel sites to developers and home sites to new residents. The unimproved land had been acquired at a nominal price by FONATUR and the increase in value of the land resulting from the development of infrastructure was to be recovered through the sale of improved parcels to hotel developers. It was projected that the income from the sale of land would be less than the costs of the infrastructure in the early stages of the project. But sales were expected to increase once Cancun matured. As an example, the initial land sales had covered only a fraction of the overall infrastructure investment associated with the first IDB loan, but it was anticipated that under the second IDB loan, there would be land sales of more than US$55 mn to offset the US$49.5 mn of infrastructure costs. The ultimate recovery of all infrastructure investment will occur near the full completion of the entire project.

The improved hotel sites, to be privately developed, could only be purchased by entities with largely Mexican ownership due to the constitutional restrictions on land ownership in coastal areas by foreigners. While this restriction had the effect of limiting achievable sales prices, it also promoted the development of management capabilities and ownership among Mexicans, which was an objective of FONATUR.

The first hotel sites were developed by private investors, but FONATUR provided much assistance via some equity participation and financing. At that time, there was little long term financing available in Mexico's capital markets because of the prevailing high inflation rate, monetary devaluations, and the high national debt. So special measures were necessary to overcome the scepticism of the private sector over the risks associated with pioneering this development. In addition, the initial land prices were kept low in order to attract investors.

As part of an effort to reduce the national debt, the financial mechanism of the debt-equity swap was introduced in the tourism sector in Mexico in the early 1980s. The swap procedure allowed a creditor to exchange his interest-bearing debt for equity in a new Mexican enterprise. From about 1983, there was a surge of creditors using the swap mechanism to take equity ownership in new hotel projects in Cancun. Mexican developers were thus able to reduce both the proportion of debt and their own equity required for hotel projects. The boom in development generated by debt-equity swaps continued until approximately 1987. It was then curtailed by more restrictive rules regarding the use of swaps in established tourism developments such as Cancun.

While FONATUR participated in the financing of several of the initial hotels, the sources of financing have increasingly diversified as Cancun has matured. The International Finance Corporation of the World Bank group, foreign banks, conventional lenders, and other national and multinational financing institutions have participated in the financing of hotels in Cancun. The government of Mexico has not provided any direct fiscal incentives to investors in tourism projects.

OVERALL EVALUATION AND CONCLUSIONS

Resort and Regional Planning

The initial resort planning was comprehensive and fundamentally sound. The primary objective of the plan — to develop a large modern integrated resort and associated service town — has essentially been achieved. The basic strengths of the plan include the adequate size of the resort area, the placement of the airport and urban zones as well as the tourism zone, the retention of conservation areas to preserve the environmentally sensitive lagoons, the planned housing and community facilities for employees, and the design details that contributed to the high standard of development desired. The design considerations encompassed the road system, the associated greenbelts, the structure of the urban and tourism zones, and the generally high standard of infrastructure.

The market analysis which supported the planning of Cancun was eventually validated by the actual international appeal of the project, especially among tourists from the USA and Canada. The market analysis underestimated the attraction of the project for domestic tourists.

While the physical planning for the urban zone was good, the planning did not accurately assess the future market for housing, nor did it fully consider the institutional framework required to implement the urban development. The goal of building a modern, efficient new town proved to be very ambitious and fraught with problems. However, these problems are being resolved and the new town is functioning satisfactorily and planning to cope with the projected continued influx of population.

Planning for the tourism zone has, by most measures, produced a successful, high quality international resort but it is sometimes criticised for its density, linear form of development, overly modern buildings and shortage of traditional style buildings. The density and linear character of development are largely due to the geography of Cancun Island, which makes it virtually imperative that hotel development be linear. Furthermore, much of the marketing success of the resort is due to the fact that many hotels have beachfront locations, which is directly attributable to the geography and form of development. Some variation of densities along Cancun Island were planned and are reflected in the varied hotel profiles. But there could perhaps have been greater differentiation of accommodation areas.

The proposed development of San Buenaventura, which is to have an historic theme that features plazas, traditional architecture, a waterfront promenade and other complementary elements, is designed to provide some contrasting design character to the resort as a counterpoint to the modern hotels. There may also be other opportunities to develop more themed areas.

The regional planning conducted as part of the Cancun project was limited but it has been beneficial. The regional infrastructure was improved by the construction of the airport, the expanded highway system, and extension of the water supply, electric and telecommunications' systems. Archaeological sites have been restored and are important attractions for tourists. Much employment was generated by the resort, providing badly needed employment for local agricultural workers in a region where agriculture was suffering, as well as for migrants from other parts of Mexico. In general, the education levels and living standards of regional residents have improved, but there have been mixed results in the housing sector because of the great in-migration of workers. The Cancun resort seems to have been a significant impetus for regional tourism development on the coast of Quintana Roo and Cozumel Island.

Development Implementation

The development of Cancun has been carried out with few major problems, despite the very substantial scope of the project. The excellent physical attributes of Cancun, its proximity to important Mayan archaeological sites, and the sizeable North American tourist markets provided a sound foundation for the project. But the manner in which it was implemented also contributed significantly to its success. There were few delays in the execution of the project and the standard of development is generally in accordance with that recommended in the initial concept. The major structural factors that facilitated the implementation process were the effective organisational framework of the implementing agencies, the financing expertise applied, and the inclusion of environmental and social considerations in the programme .

FONATUR had a specific set of objectives and the resources to fulfil those objectives. Because of its ties to the Central Bank of Mexico, FONATUR was able to mobilise the necessary technical expertise, properly fund the plan's development recommendations and undertake costly modifications to the plans when necessary. The national infrastructure agencies executed their projects satisfactorily and the state of Quintana Roo played a major role in implementing needed housing programmes. However, the less experienced municipal agencies had considerable difficulties coping with the rapid growth of the urban zone.

The financing expertise of the Central Bank and FONATUR played a major role in financing the development of Cancun. The loans from the IDB were arranged expeditiously, the required additional funds were obtained when they were needed, and the debt-equity swap mechanism was used productively to help provide the required investment in hotels.

The conservation of large tracts of land and the environmental programmes executed at Cancun have been important in retaining much of the natural character of the resort despite the considerable development that has taken place. The early social programmes were helpful in integrating the local population into the development process.

The major problem in the implementation process has been the development of the urban zone, and especially the disruptions in the orderly development of housing. The development of a large new town is an enormous undertaking which, in Cancun, encountered marketing problems and social resistance that required the joint efforts of many public agencies to overcome.

The implementation of various regional programmes has been successful. The collateral tourism development in the region has been well controlled and, as mentioned, some archaeological sites have been conserved and developed with visitor facilities. The airport appears to function well and regional highways are generally good.

Cancun has now developed about 18,000 rooms of the planned 25,000 rooms and full development is expected by the late-1990s. Completing the resort will require investment in additional infrastructure, but the principal challenge will probably continue to be the orderly development of the new town expansion necessary for the additional workers. Continued environmental monitoring, as is scheduled, will be needed to ensure that no deterioration of the environment occurs. Providing a diversity of development through themed approaches will give the resort greater architectural interest and a sense of Mexican identity.

1. FONATUR. *Cancun; Un Desarollo Turistico en la Costa Teguise.* 1982.

2. FONATUR. *Tourist Resorts: A Mexican Strategy for Development.* 1988.

3. Banco Interamericano de Desarolla. *Evaluacion Ex-Post de los Aspectos Sociales del Impacto del Proyecto de Desarollo Turistico Cancun 1.* 1979.

Chapter 5

PUERTO PLATA RESORT PROJECT DOMINICAN REPUBLIC

BACKGROUND TO THE PROJECT

Tourism in the Dominican Republic

The Dominican Republic shares the Caribbean island of Hispaniola with its western neighbour, Haiti. The country enjoys a good physical environment for tourism due to its many attractive beaches, lush mountainous terrain, several colonial forts and settlements, and tropical climate. Despite these tourist attractions, leisure tourism in the Dominican Republic was almost completely undeveloped until the late 1970s. Although an aggressive tourism incentive law was enacted in 1971, the limited infrastructure, shortage of domestic capital, uncertain political climate, and other aspects of the weak economy stifled tourism development.

There were only 779 rooms in beach hotels in 1977. During that year, 262,400 foreign tourists arrived by air, together with 47,100 Dominicans resident abroad. A further 133,400 visitors came on cruises. The few beach hotels were mainly scattered along the southeastern shore. Some of these were built by the government and the most luxurious was owned by a sugar company, largely to accommodate visitors to its own facilities. Over 80 per cent of all arrivals were from the USA in 1977, of which approximately 30 per cent were from the nearby US territory of Puerto Rico.

Since then, tourism in the country has flourished, partly as a result of the resort development initiated at Puerto Plata by the government. The Ministry of Tourism estimated that 1.2 mn foreign tourists came to the country in 1990, of which 387,588 to Puerto Plata. Estimates also indicate that the number of foreign tourists arriving by air has increased by around 14 per cent per year since 1980. The number of cruise ship arrivals has declined in recent years, from approximately 300,000 in 1980 to about 100,000 in 1989. At the end of 1989, there were almost 19,000 hotel rooms in the Dominican Republic.

The mix of tourists has increasingly diversified. A high proportion of international tourists is now from Europe, with many European visitors travelling on charter flights. According to a survey conducted by Horwath and Horwath, some 65.8 per cent of all guests in the larger hotels came for holidays and the rest for business purposes 1/. The large share of holiday visitors accounts for the longer average length of stay in Puerto Plata (8.2 nights) than in Santo Domingo (6.2 nights), which attracts more business travellers.

As is typical in most Caribbean tourist destinations, there is a marked seasonality in tourist arrivals in the Dominican Republic. Resort hotels usually enjoy average occupancy rates of over 75 per cent during the winter months of December to April and in the summer months of July and August. Occupancies in the remaining months are often below 50 per cent. The year round occupancy of large hotels was 73.2 per cent in 1989, according to the previously cited Horwath survey.

Inflation and several currency devaluations caused real room rates at the major hotels to fall from an average of US$35.00 in 1988 to US$34.80 in 1989, according to the Horwath survey. These room rates are much lower than in most other Caribbean destinations.

Domestic tourism has also grown during the past decade. There was a negligible amount of leisure tourism from the domestic market in 1980, mainly due to the low income levels of most Dominicans at the time. The proportion of domestic tourists has steadily increased, to an estimated 19.3 per cent of all the guests in the major hotels in 1989. Domestic tourism is generated primarily during holiday periods and on weekends by residents of Santo Domingo travelling to coastal resorts.

Although there has been continuous planning of selected resort centres in the Dominican Republic, there has been no formal comprehensive planning of tourism development throughout the country for many years. The focus of government efforts in tourism has been on tourism promotion, attracting investments, and other activities.

Tourism in the Puerto Plata Region

Puerto Plata is both a small city, with a population of almost 100,000, and a province on the northern coast of the Dominican Republic. The city of Puerto Plata is located at 235-km north of the capital city of Santo Domingo and, for tourists, a rather long three-hour trip from the capital. Santiago, the second most populated city in the country, is located in the northern coastal region, which has long been a major source of agricultural production and one of the most prosperous regions in the Republic.

A number of cruise ships stopped over in the harbour of the city of Puerto Plata in the 1970s. Otherwise, tourism to the region was inhibited primarily by its difficult land and air access and the fact that the northern coast is prone to rain. Thanks to a master plan for Puerto Plata, much of which has been implemented, tourism development throughout the region has since been stimulated.

The main tourist attractions of Puerto Plata are its beaches and tropical climate, although the romantic image of the Caribbean, some colonial ruins, and interesting flora and fauna in the lush mountainous terrain are of secondary interest. The climate in the region is generally equitable, with an annual mean temperature of 24.7°C (76.5°F) and only slight variations throughout the year. Most Caribbean destinations have similar attributes and are located in areas with a higher standard of infrastructure and services. Consequently, the principal unique appeal of Puerto Plata to the international travel market is the low cost of tourist goods and services.

Today, a major share of leisure tourism to the Dominican Republic is drawn to the northern coastal region. Over 32 per cent of foreign arrivals landed at the international airport at Puerto Plata in 1990. Furthermore, approximately 42 per cent of the hotel rooms in the country were in Puerto Plata in 1990. The bulk of hotel guests on the northern coast arrive by charter flights. Tourism officials estimate that 85 per cent of all room nights can be attributed to charters. Approximately 30 charter flights arrive each week at Puerto Plata airport.

Evolution of the Puerto Plata Project

The government of the Dominican Republic became interested in tourism in the late 1960s. The first of three studies on tourism authorised by the United Nations Development Programme (UNDP) was conducted in 1967. Following this study, the federal government in 1968 decreed that tourism was to be given a high priority in national development. Subsequently, the first national tourism institutions were created in 1969 and guidelines and incentives for tourism development were established in 1971.

The Central Bank of the country was given responsibilities in tourism and its president and other officials visited Mexico to investigate techniques and methods which the Central Bank of Mexico was using to address its tourism functions. Drawing on the experience of Mexico, the Central Bank formed the Departamento para el Desarrollo de la Infraestructure Turistica (INFRATUR) in 1971 to develop the infrastructure for tourism projects and aid in their financing and administration. In the same year, the construction of the airport runway at Puerto Plata was started.

A second UNDP study addressing planning issues and the viability of Puerto Plata was completed in 1972 2/. INFRATUR then carried out additional detailed studies of two resort zones, at Boca Chica along the southeast coast and at Puerto Plata. Meanwhile, a third UNDP study was conducted, which recommended that tourism development be initiated on the southeast coast because of the relatively lower infrastructure costs, drier climate and better beaches. However, after several attempts at assembling land at Boca Chica failed, that project was terminated in 1976.

Puerto Plata was selected for tourism development for a number of reasons:

• Development on the northern coast would diversify tourism geographically in the Dominican Republic.

• The required land for development was vacant and could be acquired inexpensively.

• The existing towns of Puerto Plata and Sosua offered some cultural attractions and colonial buildings, which already attracted cruise ships.

• The local residents had some experience with tourism through the established cruise business.

• There was an existing labour pool in nearby communities.

• Many Europeans fleeing the Nazi occupation had settled in the region in the 1940s and local residents were accustomed to foreigners, with some speaking German, French and English.

• The infrastructure necessary for tourism (airport, roads, etc.) would also generally benefit the north shore communities.

The leaders of the communities on the north coast actively supported the proposed tourism projects and the educated and sizeable population of the region pressed for their development.

The project proposed at Puerto Plata involved two resort complexes, one at Playa Dorada and the other at Playa Grande. Playa Dorada, located 14-km west of the airport, was intended to be developed for mass tourism while Playa Grande, at 97-km east of the city of Puerto Plata, was to target the luxury travel market. The location of these two resort complexes is shown in *Figure 10*.

Figure 10

Puerto Plata tourist region

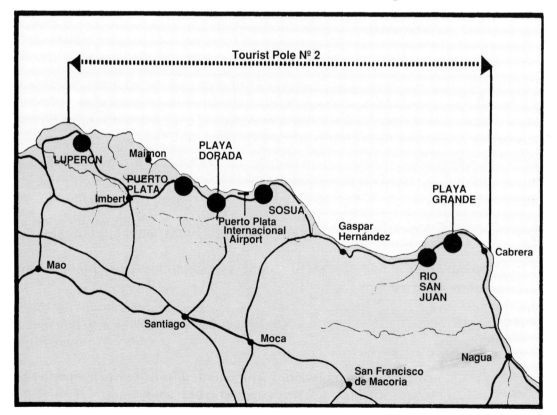

INFRATUR proceeded with the purchase of 150 hectares of undeveloped land at Playa Dorada and 300 hectares at Playa Grande and started work on construction of the infrastructure. INFRATUR then arranged an initial US$21 mn loan from the World Bank in November 1974, which helped to finance the construction of the airport terminal, part of the resort infrastructure and common facilities, and technical assistance.

It was anticipated that the development of hotels (comprising 5,200 rooms) and other commercial facilities in the resorts would be undertaken by local and foreign private investors. Most of the various elements funded by the first World Bank loan were subject to cost overruns precipitated by inflation and other factors. These additional costs were funded by INFRATUR. The airport terminal and most of the works were completed in 1980.

INFRATUR carried out an investment promotion campaign (financed by the World Bank) but was unsuccessful in attracting the necessary private investment. This was largely due to the shortage of long term financing in the Dominican Republic, the scepticism of investors regarding this pioneering project, and the unstable financial performance of hotels in Santo Domingo. Consequently, INFRATUR assumed responsibility for the development of the first of the hotels at Puerto Plata, which initially opened in 1980, together with the resort golf course. To assuage the scepticism of financiers, the project was designed and constructed to allow the alternative use of residential housing should it fail as resort accommodation. The hotel was leased to an operator who retained an option to purchase the property.

In order to overcome the shortage of long term financing, INFRATUR and the World Bank collaborated on a second loan, the main purpose of which was to finance the construction of tourist accommodation. Funds were also provided for some urban works, an artisan centre, and technical assistance. Although the financing provided by this joint World Bank/INFRATUR project was generally on favourable terms, there was still considerable reluctance among private investors. INFRATUR conducted an aggressive investment campaign which bore some fruit and a number of hotels was developed at Playa Dorada. The initial plan was modified in a number of ways as individual sites were developed. Changes were made in the number of rooms permitted, the mix of types of accommodation and the actual land uses.

While development of accommodation has progressed at Playa Dorada, the development proposed at Playa Grande has not been realised. Much of the required infrastructure has been completed but hotels have not been developed. Now that Playa Dorada is almost completed, the Central Bank is devoting its efforts to fostering tourism development at Playa Grande through the private sector.

THE RESORT PLAN AND REGIONAL CONSIDERATIONS

Resort Concept and Land Use Plan

While the Puerto Plata project encompasses two resort complexes, the focus of this study is on Playa Dorada because its plan has been largely implemented. Playa Dorada was planned as an integrated, self-contained beach resort with extensive amenities, including a golf course and convention facilities. As already mentioned, the resort was geared to the mass tourism market associated with package tours and charter flights.

The initial UNDP study of Playa Dorada was broad in scope, addressing not only infrastructure, land use, site planning and implementation, but also some regional relationships and environmental issues. Subsequently, INFRATUR refined the development plan including technical issues associated with the resort development.

An early development plan, presented in *Figure 11,* contained the following principal elements:

- 13 sites for tourist accommodation.
- An 18-hole golf course designed by Robert Trent Jones, Jr.
- A commercial centre containing convention facilities and a shopping village.
- A golf club and an equestrian school.
- A beach club aimed at the local townspeople.
- Several greenbelt reserve areas located throughout the complex.

Figure 11   **PLAYA DORADA RESORT PLAN**

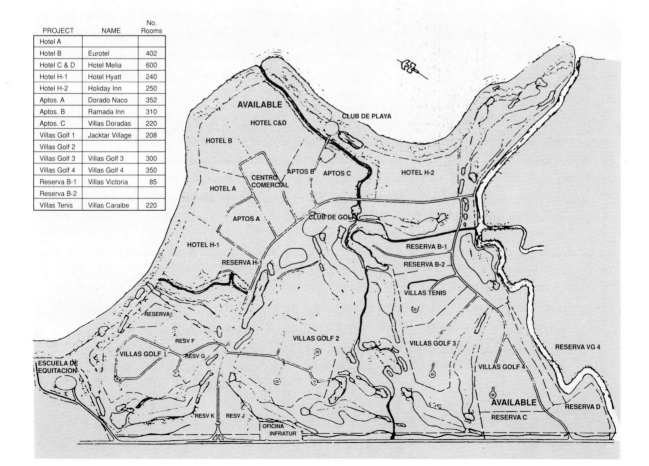

PROJECT	NAME	No. Rooms
Hotel A		
Hotel B	Eurotel	402
Hotel C & D	Hotel Melia	600
Hotel H-1	Hotel Hyatt	240
Hotel H-2	Holiday Inn	250
Aptos. A	Dorado Naco	352
Aptos. B	Ramada Inn	310
Aptos. C	Villas Doradas	220
Villas Golf 1	Jacktar Village	208
Villas Golf 2		
Villas Golf 3	Villas Golf 3	300
Villas Golf 4	Villas Golf 4	350
Reserva B-1	Villas Victoria	85
Reserva B-2		
Villas Tenis	Villas Caraibe	220

Small shacks near Punta Rucia, Puerto Plata

The Amber Museum, Puerto Plata

A view of the color-ful streets in town, Puerto Plata

Poolside view at one of
the many resorts in
Puerto Plata

Sand Castle Resort,
Puerto Plata

Coastal view of Puerto
Plata

An attraction of the 150-hectare site is its irregular coastline, which provides the opportunity for a number of interesting oceanfront lodging developments along its northern and eastern shores. The site was largely vacant prior to its acquisition by INFRATUR. It is relatively flat and has good, if not spectacular, beaches. The western boundary of the site is located on a main coastal road, which allows easy access.

The golf course was designed to occupy the centre of the resort and to buffer the project from unrelated lands on the southeastern side of the complex. The golf course also provides a landscaped setting for the interior sites that lack ocean frontage.

The infrastructure and golf course were generally developed according to the initial plan, but modifications were made in the location of accommodation, the overall density of the resort, and the type of lodging. Developments were built in areas previously designated as reserves and the planned density of the resort was increased from 3,315 to 4,768 rooms. While the initial plan called for hotel rooms to comprise 58 per cent of all rooms developed, and apartments and villas to provide the remainder, the current share of hotel accommodation is less than 20 per cent. Some design requirements for the project were established in a government decree issued in 1976. The general aim of this decree was to foster development of a high standard international resort, as recommended in the planning by INFRATUR. Key design requirements included the following:

• Shoreline setback: 60-m for all permanent structures.

• Height limit for hotels: 3 stories (11-m).

• Density for hotels: 100 beds per hectare.

• Density for residential apartments: 125 habitable rooms per hectare.

Requirements regarding outdoor lighting, landscaping, architectural style, fencing, parking, paving, utilities, various setbacks, and other aspects of development were also specified. Exceptions to all regulations can be granted by the Central Bank.

The main transportation network in Playa Dorada is provided by a loop road. A sidewalk, located mostly along the interior side of the road, accommodates pedestrian traffic. The only two entrances to the resort complex are located at each end of the loop road. This limited access promotes security in the resort but also tends to limit public access to the beaches. In addition, most of the parking is associated with the hotels and, in most of the resort, the beaches can only be reached by passing through the hotel grounds.

Infrastructure and Employee Housing

The development of the international airport at Puerto Plata helped stimulate international tourism development, as well as travel by local residents, and also encouraged the movement of goods into and out of the region. The airport, on which construction began in 1971, was subject to soil, construction and financing problems and did not begin to provide service until almost ten years later. The level of air service was initially low due to a shortage of demand. As Playa Dorada expanded, charters began to fly into Puerto Plata. But it was not until the region developed significantly that scheduled airlines began to provide frequent service. The airport facilities are generally adequate for the current level of air service, but further increases in traffic will require the development of taxiways and some minor improvements in the terminal.

With the exception of the airport project, the tourism development plan and programme did not include any other major regional infrastructure improvements. The Dominican Republic is generally considered to have inadequate infrastructure and the most noticeable shortcomings have been in roadworks, electric power, and sewage disposal. The north coast, partly as a result of the distance from Santo Domingo, has suffered even more deficiencies than other populated areas of the country. Blackouts of long duration have been common in the region and the inadequate sewage system in many populated areas has generated marine pollution. A long stretch of the coastal road near the main entrance to Playa Dorada has been unpaved for several years and the roads in the nearby tourist town of Sosua are in poor condition. Remedies to most of these problems are planned by the federal government, including the construction of a new power station in Puerto Plata, improvements to the sewage system, and road repairs. However, completion of all of these improvements may require several years. Even though the infrastructure within the resort is generally good, the deficient regional infrastructure has undoubtedly had an adverse effect on the market acceptance of Playa Dorada.

The infrastructure within Playa Dorada, which was undertaken by INFRATUR, appears to have been logically planned and generally developed to international standards. But some minor problems have become apparent in the road, electric power and sewage systems.

The loop road within Playa Dorada is two lanes which is adequate for the limited traffic currently generated by the resort. The road traffic is light because many tourists travelling on package tours use buses, guests stay mostly in the resort, and the length of stay is long which limits travel to and from the airport. Some secondary roads to clusters of accommodation are in need of repair and lack sidewalks. There is a considerable amount of pedestrian activity within the resort and the loop road contains many speed bumps in order to slow traffic. The circulation system for pedestrians could be improved. The one sidewalk is insufficient for pedestrian traffic in some areas and night lighting is inadequate in places. Vans are used to transport guests from inland accommodation to the beaches.

Electrical power is provided to Playa Dorada via underground lines which are connected to the national grid system. Electricity usage is not measured and the charges incurred by the accommodation and other facility enterprises therefore do not vary with usage, but are fixed.

The independent sewage collection and treatment system for the resort was developed to the standards then required by the World Bank. Treated sewage is discharged through sea outfalls. The system is sometimes overloaded during periods of heavy rain.

The remaining infrastructure generally functions adequately. The potable water is treated in an independent system built to World Bank standards, and a standby connection to the regional system can supply water in emergencies. Telephone service is underground at the resort and a new microwave station that links Puerto Plata with Santo Domingo and the international communications network was recently installed. Modern equipment for the collection of solid waste is employed at Playa Dorada, and the solid waste is transported to regional disposal sites. An ongoing insect abatement programme is conducted at and near the resort in collaboration with the Public Health Department.

Many employees working in the resort live in the city of Puerto Plata, which is located at less than 5-km from Playa Dorada. No housing was specifically built for employees. Bus service is provided for those employees who commute from the city.

Economic Impact Analysis

All the different project analyses conducted by the World Bank found the project to be economically viable. The first comprehensive analysis of the proposed project projected an estimated internal rate of return of 17.5 per cent and a subsequent post-project analysis yielded a lower but still satisfactory rate of return. In its initial analysis, the World Bank estimated that the project would yield foreign exchange earnings of US$74 mn by 1988 and annual government receipts of US$7 mn when all tax holidays had expired. One important economic impact of the resort was also expected to be the stimulation of regional development, which has indeed been a successful result of the project.

The employment generated by the project is significant. The World Bank estimated that the construction of only the superstructure would generate over 10,000 man-years of employment and that the total permanent employment from the project would exceed 8,000 jobs. In addition, unskilled labour would benefit particularly, since the wages in the tourism sector are higher than in alternative jobs for unskilled labourers.

Regional Relationships

As already mentioned, the international airport at Puerto Plata was the most important regional infrastructure improvement and some major roads in the northern region were improved. However, while the development at Playa Dorada is well planned and some development controls have been applied on north coast tourism included in the Puerto Plata project, much of the tourism development that has taken place in the region has obvious shortcomings.

The small town of Sosua, which is located near several good beaches, has become a centre for retail tourist shops and budget accommodation. But its infrastructure, especially its road network, is inadequate to serve the commercial activity.

Tourism development is scattered along the coast on the fringes of towns and sometimes lies adjacent to land that is incompatible. In one case, an entire neighbourhood is being relocated by government authorities to accommodate additional tourism development and to remedy a deficient sewage system that is polluting recreational beaches.

In addition, a large number of incompleted tourism projects have been postponed or abandoned in the region and there is considerable land speculation. Along some beaches, tourism related structures have been built that protrude onto the sand. Effective regional planning that considers and controls the recent explosive growth of tourism is still needed.

DEVELOPMENT IMPLEMENTATION

Organisation and Responsibilities for Resort Implementation

INFRATUR, established to foster the development of tourism throughout the Dominican Republic, was charged with the design and construction of all infrastructure and common facilities required for the Puerto Plata project. When the development of the superstructure at Playa Dorada lagged, INFRATUR assumed the responsibility for the arrangement of financing and supervision of the development of accommodation and related facilities and activities.

As already indicated, INFRATUR was formed as a subsidiary of the Central Bank to ensure full funding of its endeavours, to obtain the support of international lending agencies, and to remove political considerations from the development process. When the Puerto Plata project was initiated, the governing body of INFRATUR was a board that was chaired by the Governor of the Central Bank and included as members the Manager of the Central Bank, its legal counsel, a member of the Monetary Board, and the director of the predecessor agency to the Ministry of Tourism. One of the initial problems of INFRATUR was continuity of management. There were reportedly eight directors during the the first five years of the organisation.

INFRATUR had two operating divisions, one of which was responsible for the development of the infrastructure and enforcement of design controls at

Puerto Plata, and the other division was in charge of the financing arranged principally for the construction of the required superstructure. When little interest was expressed in the development of the first hotels at Playa Dorada, INFRATUR also assumed the responsibility for the development of the initial accommodation projects.

INFRATUR retained international consultants to work in conjunction with local consultants and the technical staff of INFRATUR in the design and supervision of the development of the infrastructure and resort facilities. The involvement of international consultants declined as the project matured.

INFRATUR was responsible for the development of the infrastructure, a handicrafts centre, and other components of the project. On completion, the infrastructure was to be purchased by the appropriate utility or public authority which would then operate it and charge the user fees. INFRATUR continues to supervise the operations and remaining development in Playa Dorada. The Central Bank has assumed responsibility for Playa Grande and is investigating its sale to private developers.

Having accomplished its task of spurring the growth of tourism in the north shore region, INFRATUR now has considerably fewer functions than in past years. Because of this situation, there has been talk of disbanding the organisation.

Resort Development Programming

The initial project schedule prepared by INFRATUR, which was based on the UNDP planning study completed in 1972, was not met. This was largely due to the lack of sufficient financing — not an unusual situation during the conceptual stages of resort development projects. Subsequently, many development schedules were prepared throughout the formulation and execution of the Puerto Plata project, but the major commitments were made by INFRATUR when the two World Bank loans were arranged.

The first World Bank loan (for the infrastructure and airport terminal) was approved in November 1974 but the airport did not open until 1980, much later than programmed. As mentioned, this delay was largely due to unexpected adverse soil condition at the airport and to inflationary increases in the cost of the infrastructure that required additional funding by INFRATUR. Subsequently, no private investors came forward to construct the accommodation facilities and the project was again delayed.

The second World Bank loan (mainly for a credit line for the development of the accommodation) was approved in 1979 and the terms of the loan required that commitments be obtained for all the lodging projects within three years (by 1982) and that all construction be completed within five years (by 1984). This schedule was not met, either. It appears to have been too ambitious in that it did not allow sufficient time for the required steps of attracting investors, arranging financing, and the design and construction of the accommodation. In addition, the schedule called for the development of as many as 1,600 rooms in a very short period, which may have generated some market resistance and would have strained the capacity of the construction industry.

The interest of hotel entrepreneurs in this pioneering project remained tepid until the investment promotional campaign was launched and innovative financing schemes began to generate momentum. When the initial accommodation was opened, a number of investors emerged and the development of Playa Dorada proceeded rapidly.

Regional Plan Implementation

While there is some planning conducted in the provincial offices of Puerto Plata, it is very general and the provincial government has insufficient enforcement powers. There is little public participation in the planning process. The federal government accorded INFRATUR some powers to control aspects of tourism development on the north coast, mainly in a decree issued in 1976. Subsequently, a zoning plan was prepared in 1984. As indicated, the Puerto Plata project did not include regional planning and development to any great extent.

Enforcement of the existing regional development controls has been difficult because the regional planning efforts are not sufficiently comprehensive and detailed, and decision-making on development proposals frequently becomes politicised. The review process also suffered during periods when there were frequent changes in the administration of INFRATUR. Consequently, problems surfaced in Sosua and the development along the coast took place in a scattered and disorganised manner.

Education and Training of Resort Employees

A hotel school was founded in Puerto Plata in 1978. It offers primarily technical training for entry-level employees in front office operations, catering, housekeeping, property maintenance, and other aspects of hotel operations. Training in foreign languages is also provided and many hotel employees have conversational skills in English. The training programmes are of six months, one year and 18 months in length. The number of students in this programme is low because of the shortage of educational materials and the generally limited attendance in schools in the Dominican Republic where formal education is not mandatory and literacy rates are low.

A small local Catholic University recently began to offer a programme in hotel administration. The University has a critical shortage of instructional materials and this programme is only developing slowly. There are several university and vocational tourism programmes in Santo Domingo and some aspiring employees from the north coast move to Santo Domingo to attend these schools.

Current Status of Development

Only a few undeveloped sites remain for accommodation facilities at Puerto Plata. Thirteen sites were provided in the initial plans but additional accommodation has been built on three sites which were originally designated as reserves. On the present 16 sites, there are 12 hotels in operation, one under construction, and three sites are vacant (Table 3). Of the undeveloped sites, two have excellent beachfront locations. The higher prices of these parcels of land has apparently discouraged their development.

All the accommodation has been built to international standards. As indicated in the table, many are apartment hotels which feature large suite rooms. Some of the facilities offer inclusive package rates for room and food (American Plan). The golf course and infrastructure are fully completed. The commercial centre, which contains a convention centre and retail facilities, is under construction.

The market mix of tourists in Playa Dorada, initially expected to be dominated by North Americans, is currently largely European. A number of competitive resort destinations in the Caribbean, including Puerto Rico and Cancun, have attracted major shares of the North American market. In addition, marketing resort destinations in the fragmented travel industry of North America requires significant resources, which both the Dominican Republic and the hotels at Playa Dorada lack. None of the accommodation facilities in Puerto Dorada has an affiliation with a North American hotel chain. In contrast, the travel industry in Europe is concentrated among several major tour operators. Attracting their business is easier and is greatly influenced by the price and value of the ground package. Moreover, the package tours originating in Europe are typically of two weeks in length while those from the USA are usually only one week long. The Ministry of Tourism and the hotel operators at Playa Dorada were able to achieve this shift in marketing emphasis in a remarkably short and effective fashion.

Most of the European tourists purchase package tours and come to Playa Dorada on charter flights. As a result, the negotiated room rates are often low and the yield is also low, even though occupancies may be good. Some of the more recently developed facilities, which do not have subsidised financing, are experiencing financial problems. Consequently, much of the investors' interest in the planned undeveloped sites has lagged.

As indicated previously, the infrastructure has been completed at the second planned resort complex, Playa Grande, but the development of accommodation has not materialised. This resort site is now being offered for sale to the private sector.

Socio-Economic and Environmental Impact

At the present time, the direct economic benefits of Playa Dorada may be close to those projected by the World Bank. It was anticipated that 2,965 rooms would be

Table 3:
Current status of hotel development in Puerto Plata

Facility	Rooms/units	Type of facility
Existing		
Playa Dorada Hotel	252	Hotel (former Holiday Inn)
Eurotel	402	Beachfront hotel
Dorado Naco I	204	Apartment hotel - Phase I
Flamenco Beach Resort	322	Apartment hotel
Villas Doradas	207	Apartment hotel
Jack Tar Village	300	Bungalow style villas
Puerto Plata Village	504	Inland golf villas
Princess Playa Dorada	336	Inland golf villas
Villas Victoria	120	Inland golf villas
Tropicana Caribe	168	Inland golf villas
Heavens	150	Inland golf villas
Village Caribe	240	Inland tennis villas
Total existing units	<u>3,205</u>	
Under Construction		
Dorado Naco II	428	Apartment hotel Phase II
Planned		
Hotel site A	295	Beachfront hotel
Hotel sites C and D	590	Beachfront hotel
Golf Villas IV	250	Inland villas
Total planned units	<u>1,563</u>	
TOTAL ALL UNITS	4,768	

built by 1990, but 3,205 rooms have actually been constructed. The existing development generates an estimated 5,100 jobs in the resort, based on the staff to room ratio of 1.6 that prevails on the north coast. In addition, there is an unidentifiable amount of employment outside the resort in the supply sector. However, the hotels' profitability is adversely affected by the average room rates which were lower than expected. Eventually, the economic benefits of the resort may be much greater than anticipated when additional development takes place on the remaining sites.

The Puerto Plata project has had a major impact on the national, regional and local economies. The national benefits of this tourism project include significant incremental economic development, the generation of foreign exchange, considerable employment generation, sectoral diversification, and the dispersal of development to less populated areas.

One main purpose of the project was to encourage regional economic development, and this has been successful overall. The regional impact of this project is substantial, with the project being largely responsible for the development of the tourism sector on the north coast. Without this project, it is likely that tourism in the region would have remained a minor activity characterised by a few cruise ship stopovers and some budget travel. Instead, the construction of around 3,000 rooms at Playa Dorada and the supporting infrastructure generated the collateral development of the bulk of the additional 15,000 rooms now existing in the province of Puerto Plata. Tourism has become a major economic activity in the region, generating income and employment both for those directly employed in tourism and those supported in tourism supply activities. In addition, travel by local residents and the transport of goods were facilitated by the development of the international airport that was built mainly for tourism.

As a result, the national and regional economic benefits of the project are far greater than originally anticipated because of the stimulus given to collateral tourism development. But as already explained, much of the tourism development outside the resort project area is environmentally not well planned and controlled, and some problems such as land speculation are occurring.

Because of the careful planning and application of development controls, the Playa Dorada resort was developed to much higher environmental standards than most of the other accommodation projects on the north coast. But the development of three additional accommodation sites in areas originally designated as reserves has increased the overall density of the project and altered its visual impact.

One major environmental problem is the beach erosion that has occurred along the northern shore, especially in front of the Eurotel hotel. This formerly wide beach has virtually disappeared and sand bags have been placed around the foundations of some restaurant buildings to protect them from wave damage. Tourism officials are not certain of the cause of this erosion. Some indicate that recent storms are at fault while others point to the destruction of near-shore reefs with dynamite that was reportedly used to enlarge the swimming area in front of the hotel.

The Puerto Plata project itself appears to have had a largely positive socio-cultural impact. This is due to the increase in employment and income and consequent rise in living standards of employees and their families directly or indirectly supported by tourism. Only a minor negative impact can be ascribed to the resort development because residents had already been exposed to foreign tourists through the cruise ship stopovers. INFRATUR included funds for the identification and mitigation of social impact in the first World Bank loan.

Puerto Plata did, however, induce the development of much additional tourism throughout the region, which has certainly generated significant socio-cultural impact. The favourable impact generated by increased employment and income are evident as there is some migration to Puerto Plata and Sosua from rural areas and Haiti. It appears that this migration has generated little negative impact, especially when compared with the explosive growth of the population of Santo Domingo. The composition of the labour force is changing as the proportion of employment in agriculture has declined in favour of the service sector, and especially tourism. These changes seem to have caused some modification of traditional values, which may be considered desirable or undesirable depending on standards of evaluation.

FINANCING OF PLANNING AND DEVELOPMENT

The funding for the early planning was provided by the Central Bank (after 1971, through its subsidiary of INFRATUR) and the UNDP. All subsequent detailed planning was funded by INFRATUR.

The development of the infrastructure was started by the federal government but most of the funding was provided jointly by INFRATUR and the World Bank (which issued a loan for US$21 mn). It was anticipated that the completed infrastructure would then be purchased by the appropriate utility or other public entity which would operate it and collect user fees. In practice, the utilities seldom had sufficient resources to fully reimburse INFRATUR and the completed infrastructure was usually transferred for little, if any, return.

A major source of revenue to repay these loans for infrastructure development was intended to be the sale of accommodation sites to developers. The land had been acquired by INFRATUR at a nominal price and the increase in value generated by the development was to be recovered through the sale of improved sites. However, the site sale prices covered only a fraction of the overall investment. At some point, the sale of Playa Grande may provide an additional return but it is unlikely that the full investment will be directly recovered. However, the annual taxes and other government revenues attributable to tourism on the north coast will provide an indirect return on investment.

It was anticipated that the funding for accommodation facilities would be provided mainly by the private sector. In addition, government entities including

INFRATUR had been making hotel loans in Santo Domingo and could therefore be a source for some loans. This was not the case. Private lenders did not materialise and even many of the loans made for hotel development in Santo Domingo had defaulted. To overcome this obstacle, INFRATUR, the World Bank and commercial banks collaborated on a loan, the main purpose of which was to fund the development of the tourism superstructure in Puerto Plata.

Table 4:
Total participation of lenders and equity investors in Playa Dorada accommodation projects

Lender	Amount (US$ mn)
INFRATUR	10
World Bank	25
Foreign commercial banks	10
Dominican Republic commercial banks	2
Equity investors	24
Total	71

This complicated financing mechanism was not arranged without difficulties. Each loan participant had special requirements over the use of funds and loan guarantees. In general, the Central Bank issued full government guarantees for all borrowing. This financial approach was required because of the difficult financing market then prevailing in the Dominican Republic. While a shortage of long term funds is common in developing countries, the problems of this particular situation were compounded by investor scepticism over pioneering hotels on the north coast, as well as the financial problems being experienced by hotels in Santo Domingo.

The hotels developed initially at Playa Dorada were constructed with innovative financing approaches. The first property was built by INFRATUR and then leased to an operator who retained an option to purchase it, thereby allowing much of the development risk to be shared by INFRATUR. Many subsequent facilities were built as condominium projects, with individual units sold to private investors who retained rights to use the units for a limited period each year and leased the unit to the management company or entered into a rental pool arrangement. These condominium operations are generating some controversy among the owners of the units who claim that their proper share of revenues are not being paid.

All but a few of the hotel projects at Playa Dorada were funded with the INFRATUR/World Bank credit facility. The World Bank actually contributed only US$21.5 mn of its obligation, partly because there were no loan applications submitted for accommodation projects scheduled for Playa Grande.

The individual loans to hotel developers were issued by financial intermediaries who assumed full credit risk. The project loans typically had a loan term of 17 years, a grace period (requiring no debt payments) of as many as four years, an interest rate of 12 per cent, and some loan fees. The project loans could represent 65 per cent of costs. Investors were required to contribute the remaining 35 per cent in equity. These loans eventually became windfalls for the borrowers as inflation and devaluations reduced the real value of debt repayments. Not surprisingly, there have been no loan defaults.

A financing arrangement of US$50 mn for accommodation projects was also negotiated with the Inter-American Development Bank (IDB), but problems with the terms and implementing agencies have caused it to go unused.

On the termination of the INFRATUR/World Bank credit facilitation, the last few hotels in Playa Dorada were built with funds from commercial lenders at market rates. Owing to the high rates of inflation, the interest rates increased dramatically, thereby placing severe financial strains on the borrowers. Many of these last few projects may fail or require some refinancing.

The very generous fiscal incentives available to investors in tourism projects in the Dominican Republic include:

• Full exemption from income taxes for a period of ten years, with a possible extension for a further five years.
• Exemption from construction taxes, corporate taxes and national and municipal taxes on licenses and public events.

• Exemption from import duties and taxes on imported goods for construction and operations if local goods are unavailable.

The extent to which these incentives have induced investment in tourism projects is unclear.

OVERALL EVALUATION AND CONCLUSIONS

Resort and Regional Planning

Although there have been a few problems, Playa Dorada has become a reasonably successful resort, partly because of its generally well conceived plan. The integration of the golf course, the good design of circulation, the incorporation of extensive ocean setbacks, the spacious accommodation sites, and other features provide an attractive resort complex. There were modifications in the original plan that increased density but these changes did not greatly affect the character of the resort.

The plan to promote Playa Dorada as a destination for mass tourism was fortuitous. Charter flights brought large numbers of tourists to Puerto Plata when the shortage of scheduled flights could not. The limited marketing budgets of the hotels did not greatly inhibit the penetration of the mass tourism market as it would have other market segments. Moreover, when the North American market dissipated, it was quickly replaced with the European market, which would have been very difficult if the resort was not geared to charters and package tours.

The plan for the whole of Puerto Plata, which recommended the near simultaneous development of both Playa Dorada and Playa Grande, proved to be faulty. It ignored the typical gravitational expansion pattern of resort tourism, which prevails in a relatively small region, whereby tourism development expands outward from an established core in a sequential pattern. Tourism development does not normally develop simultaneously in two major relatively nearby centres, unless there are severe natural or artificially imposed restraints to suppress intermediate development. In the case of the north coast of the Dominican Republic, there are no major natural barriers and, in the absence of strong regional planning controls, artificial restrictions did not exist. In addition, the higher quality market aimed for at Playa Grande has not materialised in the country.

The greatest contribution of the Playa Dorada project has perhaps been the economic development, especially of collateral tourism development, that it stimulated throughout the region. However, the weak regional planning and implementation has not only reduced the economic benefits but has also generated some adverse environmental and socio-cultural impact. One particular problem has been the deficient regional infrastructure, notably in electricity and roads.

Development Implementation

The organisation in charge of the development of tourism on the north coast, INFRATUR, was given extensive responsibilities that included not only the development of the resort complexes of Playa Dorada and Playa Grande, but also important functions throughout the 200-km stretch of coastline designated as the Puerto Plata tourism zone. INFRATUR, as a subsidiary of the Central Bank, had the necessary funding and expertise in lending to execute the important financing functions. It added technical planning, construction, and project administration expertise through the employment of consultants and hiring of local professionals. This organisation was well structured but it functioned less effectively during periods when management changes were frequent.

The organisation of financing for both infrastructure and hotels greatly affected the timing and extent of the implementation of Playa Dorada. Initial planning underestimated the difficulties associated with the financing of the accommodation. When the financing was in place, the implementation of the main components of the project proceeded rapidly and largely according to plan. The few shortcomings in the implementation process occurred mainly in the regional context, and perhaps in the control over the construction and operating practices of individual hotel projects.

While the infrastructure in Playa Dorada was built to high standards, the problems associated with the regional infrastructure had a major effect on the implementation process. The lack of a regular supply of electricity and a generally poor quality road system negatively affected the marketing of tourism, the interest of potential accommodation investors, and other aspects of tourism development on the north coast.

The significant tourism development that took place on the north coast outside Playa Dorada, although of great economic benefit, generated some problems. INFRATUR was given some functional responsibilities for the control of this regional development but, without a comprehensive regional plan and an effective regulatory mechanism to overcome the political issues associated with many of the individual developments, the control of regional development could not be maintained.

Most of the individual hotels in Playa Dorada are attractive and provide a good holiday experience, as demonstrated by the favourable guest satisfaction indicated in tourist surveys. On the other hand, some of the operating practices of condominium apartment managers appear to have generated some discontent among condominium owners. These problems do not prevail in the operation of traditional type hotels, which also typically generate greater visitor spending.

Of significant concern regarding the long term potential of Playa Dorada is the beach erosion that has occurred. Whatever the cause, this condition requires investigation and corrective action.

In general, the Playa Dorada resort was a successful initial development that established holiday tourism on the north coast of the Dominican Republic. In retrospect, there was a need for more comprehensive and detailed regional planning and development controls.

The development taking place outside Playa Dorada in the region suggests that continued planning and application of land use and project development controls on the north coast are required, in order to reinforce the achievements of the resort project. Such an approach would focus on the careful monitoring of future development and the adoption of measures to correct existing problems along with providing much needed infrastructure improvements.

---

1. Horwath & Horwath. *La Industria Hotelera Dominicana en Cifras: 1990.*

2. Shankland Cox & Assoc. *Tourism Development Study - Puerto Plata.* 1972.

Chapter 6

SOUTH ANTALYA TOURISM DEVELOPMENT PROJECT TURKEY

The four preceding case studies dealt with the planning of integrated resort developments in specifically bounded areas, where the entire sites were used for tourism related purposes. The South Antalya Tourism Development Project, in contrast, is an excellent example of a major tourism development in a large area which includes existing communities, agriculture, and extensive forest and parks. As a result, an important planning task was to integrate tourism regionally, both within the project area and to places outside the area that are linked to South Antalya. As was the case with the other studies, effective organisational and financial approaches were essential in determining the ultimate success of the resort development.

BACKGROUND

Tourism in Turkey

Turkey covers a relatively large and environmentally diverse land area with long coastlines on the Mediterranean, Aegean and Black Seas, a population of more than 55 mn, and a long history with many cultural influences that reflect its geographic location bridging Europe and the Middle East. The country offers a great diversity of natural, historic and cultural attractions for tourists. There was limited development of tourism in the 1970s but this was followed by rapid growth during the 1980s — from 1.6 mn international visitor arrivals in 1983 to 5.4 mn in 1990 1/. Growth was especially strong during the latter part of the decade. The rapid growth of tourism reflects the accelerated development of tourist facilities, services and related infrastructure and the increasing international awareness of the attractions and facilities available in the country.

Tourism contributes significantly to Turkey's national economy. In 1990, international tourism receipts totalled US$3,346 mn. The previous year — the most recent year for which detailed information is available — tourist receipts accounted for 22 per cent of Turkey's total export earnings and 3.2 per cent of the country's gross national product (GNP). It provided some 142,700 jobs in hotels, restaurants, travel agencies, tour operators and the public sector.

As a result of the expanding economy of Turkey, domestic tourism is also becoming fairly important. In the late 1980s, the estimated number of domestic tourist nights generated by the domestic market was close to 50 per cent of the international bednight total.

The major foreign market for Turkey is Western Europe which accounted for 53.4 per cent of total arrivals in 1990. Germany heads the ranking, accounting for 18.1 per cent of all arrivals, followed by the UK, France, Greece, Austria, Italy, Sweden and Finland. Eastern Europe generated 27.1 per cent of arrivals in 1990, with Romania, Yugoslavia, the USSR, Poland and Hungary as the major sources from that region. Other significant sources of tourism are the USA (2.8 per cent) and Syria (2.1 per cent) while Canada, Australia and Japan are important growth markets, albeit from smaller bases. In 1989, 52.6 per cent of international visitors to Turkey arrived by air, 28.9 per cent by road, 16.7 per cent by sea and the remainder by rail. More than 90 per cent of visitors are travelling on holiday. Yachting tourism is becoming popular in Turkey and in 1988, almost 21,000 yachtsmen and their crews spent at least one night in the country.

Seasonality is very marked, with May to October being the peak arrivals season. The months March/April and November/December are the shoulder months and visitor arrivals fall sharply in January/February. The peak month of August accounts for about seven times more arrivals than the lowest month of January. The average length of stay in the country is between 9-10 nights. In 1989, the average expenditure per foreign tourist was US$570. Tourism contributes a very positive balance to Turkey's tourism account as expenditure by Turks on international tourism falls well short of international tourist receipts.

The development of tourism in Turkey started with the creation of the Ministry of Tourism in 1965, and the preparation of tourism development plans in the late 1960s and 1970s. Since then, detailed tourism planning has continued to be an important part of the government's overall strategic planning. Tourism has been a particularly high priority since the early 1980s and the adoption of the Tourism Encouragement Law in 1982. The South Antalya area and other regions in Southwest Turkey and elsewhere were designated for tourism development during this early period of planning.

Tourism is included as a sector in the national five-year development plans. By the end of the current sixth national plan period (1990-1994), international tourist arrivals are targeted to reach 7.4 mn a year, representing an annual growth rate of 8.2 per cent, and international tourist receipts are projected to reach US$5,514 mn. Total tourist bed capacity is expected to exceed 350,000 beds by 1994, compared with 145,000 beds in 1989. The tourism policies and principles adopted for the sixth plan period are as follows 2/:

• Incentive policies will be improved to make specific sectors of tourism more attractive, notably winter tourism, hunting and water sports, festivals, health, youth, the congress market, thermal tourism, golf and third age tourism.

• The number of people employed in the tourism sector, either directly or indirectly, will be increased to an adequate level and their knowledge and skills will be enhanced through training programmes.

• Importance will be attached to the improved quality of tourism and the growth in infrastructure capacity.

One of the tourist
hotels along the South
Antalya coast, tourist
development area

South Antalya coast

Paradise Albeach Golf
Hotel, Belek, Antalya

Panoramic view of
Side, eastern part of
South Antalya coast,
the ancient theater

Ancient temple of
Apollo situated in Side

Club Mega Saray
holiday village is one of
the several holiday
facilities on the Belek
coast of Antalya

• Preservation of the cultural and natural heritage will be a high priority and tourism activities and investments will be planned and implemented according to approved environmental and landscaping minimum standards.

• Charter travel will be developed and domestic tour operations encouraged.

• Measures will be taken to increase hotel average occupancy rates, to extend the tourist season, and to improve the quality of existing properties.

• Priority will be given to the conservation of natural and cultural attractions; designated areas will be preserved and promoted for tourism.

• Hotel management expertise will be developed, and the development of low capacity and family managed properties will be encouraged.

• Citizens will be given opportunities to take their holidays at their convenience and in a healthy environment.

Tourism in South Antalya

The South Antalya region, which comprises the resort development project examined in this study, extends for some 80-km south of Antalya city along the Mediterranean coast in southwestern Turkey. Antalya city is outside the project area but is the major city of the entire Antalya region, where the airport serving the region is located. It provides its own attractions of a well developed, attractive and highly scenic tourist-oriented harbour environment, historic districts, buildings and structures including ancient walls and gates, important religious monuments, shopping facilities, and an archaeological museum. There has been considerable development of accommodation and other tourist facilities in Antalya city, including some very interesting renovated historic hotels and guest houses. Thus, the city functions as the gateway to both the south and east Antalya tourism areas, as well as providing attractions which are visited by tourists staying in both the South Antalya project area and the newly developing East Antalya tourism area. *Figure 12* depicts the entire Antalya region and its main attractions.

Within the South Antalya project area, attractions for tourists include the very scenic coastal area of mountains situated near the shoreline, a narrow coastal plain, good beaches, archaeological and historic sites, and traditional Turkish villages and architecture. Some specific scenic and natural sites are open to tourists. Recognition on the part of government that this scenic beauty needed to be preserved has led to the entire region, including the project area, being designated, planned and developed as the Olympus Seashore National Park.

The South Antalya tourism area is focused on the town of Kemer on Kemer Bay, which has a long history dating back to the Greek Homeric period. Olympus, founded during the 3rd century BC, and two other ancient city sites, Phaselis and Idyros, are located in South Antalya. In addition to the main town of Kemer, there are six other villages in the area. In the heavily wooded surroundings of Kemer Bay, there are existing tourist holiday villages and a major marina serving the

Figure 12

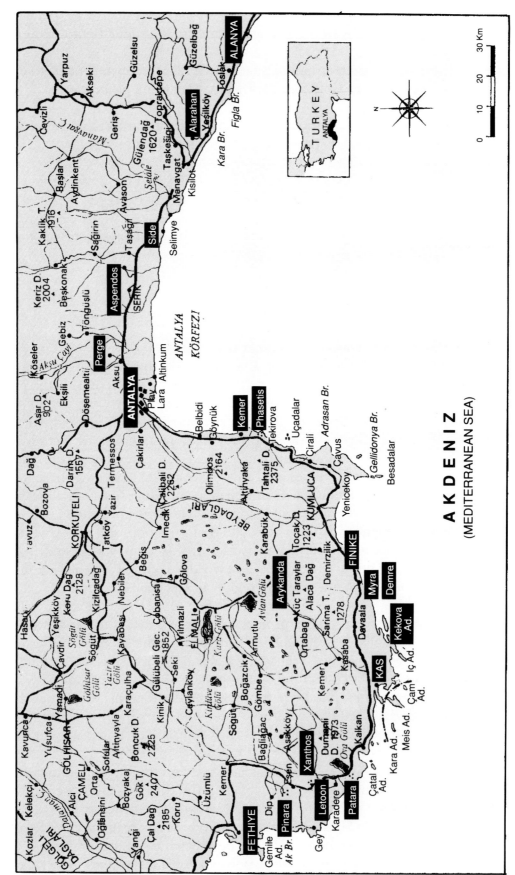

88

entire area has been developed on the bay in the town. Before the tourism project commenced, South Antalya was not very developed, either in general or tourism terms, and the population living in the area was limited. At that time, there was no incorporated municipality. As recorded in the 1980 census, the total population in the South Antalya region was about 10,000.

Evolution of the South Antalya Project

In 1969, the government decided that tourism should be developed and the southwest coastal region of the country extending 200-km inland was designated for tourism, with no development allowed until planning was completed. Initial planning received international assistance and expertise from France, Scandinavia and other sources. In addition to the southwest region, some cultural sites including Cappadocia in central Turkey were added to the planning programme. In the southwest, structural plans on a scale of 1:200,000 were first formulated, identifying the tourism area boundaries, the tourism development zones and other related areas such as historic and natural sites, forest areas, settlement areas, and the transportation network of airports, roads and marinas. Plans on a scale of 1:25,000 were then drawn up for the tourism development areas including South Antalya, and 1:1,000-scale plans have been prepared for specific development sites.

From 1974 to 1976, an integrated tourism plan and related feasibility studies were prepared and adopted for South Antalya as well as some other tourism areas, and the World Bank (International Bank for Reconstruction and Development - IBRD, and the International Development Association - IDA) was approached for financial and technical assistance. An IDA credit for about US$26 mn was approved to cover the foreign exchange component of the infrastructure development, and the loan agreement was signed in September 1976. The Ministry of Tourism was the agency designated for the overall execution of the project and it, in turn, appointed the Tourism Bank to undertake project development. The South Antalya Tourism Development Project was included in the Government Public Investment Projects list in 1976 and, in 1978, was included in the list of priority projects. The acquisition of land, where necessary, and the development of the infrastructure started in the late 1970s.

The South Antalya tourism project is considered by the government to be the most successful tourism development project in Turkey incorporating, from its outset, integrated planning, programming, financing and operation.

THE SOUTH ANTALYA PLAN AND REGIONAL CONSIDERATIONS

Resort Concept and Land Use Plan

The tourism plan for South Antalya is a regional or sub-regional plan which indicates major development areas for tourism, town and village settlements, forest areas to be preserved, major archaeological/historic sites, the road network and a large marina. The overall plans for South and East Antalya are shown in *Figure 13*, and the northern part of the South Antalya plan, where Kemer and the accommodation areas are located, is reproduced in *Figure 14 3/*. The red colour on the maps identifies the proposed tourist accommodation areas. Some minor plan changes have been made since this particular map was produced, but the planning concept remains the same. Within the framework of this regional plan, a more detailed plan has been prepared for the region 4/, as well as for Kemer town and its surroundings, which includes beach tourism areas 5/.

The original plan called for a capacity of 25,000 beds in the area surveyed by the World Bank which, after an amendment was made to the plan, was adjusted upwards to 58,000 beds. A more recent amendment to the plan in 1990 indicates a 65,500 bed capacity in the whole of South Antalya, including a new development site at Adrasan Bay, a considerable distance south of the main concentration of development in the Kemer area. Accommodation includes a large number of holiday villages and some hotels, camping sites and guest houses. In addition, current policy is to encourage owner managed, small-scale accommodation and traditional hotels where permitted on the plan. Tourism development in South Antalya is aimed primarily at international tourists (80 per cent of all tourists to the area), in order to generate foreign exchange earnings.

The land use concept of the regional plan is to develop Kemer as the tourism service centre of South Antalya, with a relatively large marina, associated hotel and restaurant complex and other tourist facilities. These include a hotel school and training hotel, information centre, medical clinic, fire fighting station, the resort development office, employee housing, tour and travel agencies and other commercial tourist facilities, small-scale hotels, guest houses and self-catering units, all integrated into the existing community. Close to Kemer is the archaeological site of Idyros. The hotel and holiday village accommodation sites are beach-oriented and mainly located near or within a few km of Kemer. The only remote accommodation site is the one recently added to the plan and scheduled for 6,700 beds, located on Adrasan Bay.

The 1990 plan also included two 18-hole golf courses, camping sites, day use picnicking and recreation areas, 11 entertainment centres designed to attract tourists inland from the coast, and a health-oriented tourism centre. The existing villages are separated from the accommodation sites and allow sufficient space on the plan for expansion. The main coastal road provides good access to Kemer, which is close by — but not divided by — the main road and the accommodation sites, as well as most of the existing villages and ancient city ruins. The remainder of the region is designated for agriculture and preserved forest and is, as mentioned, all part of the Olympus Seashore National Park. Specific sites of archaeological, scenic and natural interest are also designated. Several water conservation and breeding zones are indicated on the plan. In addition to the tourism plan, a master plan has been prepared for the national park and is being implemented.

Development and design standards have been specified and are applied to tourism development. The minimum setback of buildings from the beach vegetation line is 20-m (except in Kemer town). The maximum height of buildings is five stories (16.5-m) and lower for holiday villages. Maximum land coverage by buildings is 15-20 per cent, and floor area ratios are 20, 30 or 40 per cent depending on the type of development. Existing trees on the development sites must be retained as far as possible and for each tree that is removed, three new trees must be planted on the site. Access corridors to the shoreline are shown on the plan and some public beach parks have been designated. Each detailed plan for the accommodation areas includes specific development controls and design guidelines. Some of the holiday villages incorporate traditional Turkish design layouts and architectural motifs.

Infrastructure and Employee Housing

Infrastructure planning and development for South Antalya included roads, water supply, electric power, sewage and solid waste collection and disposal, telecommunications, the yacht marina, medical clinic, fire protection, and other facilities and services. Although not part of the immediate tourism project, improvements to the airport near Antalya city, which was formerly a military airfield, were carried out by the government in large part to serve the South Antalya project. The state highway to serve the area from Antalya city was developed, as were secondary roads. A potable water supply was developed from a mountain source to serve the accommodation sites and nearby rural areas. The town of Kemer was provided with an 18-km water supply network, and the total water distribution network encompasses 90 km. Town roads were improved. An 13-km sewage collection system was constructed in the town and a network of sewer lines developed to serve various accommodation areas. Sewage treatment is carried out at about four plants in the area to a high level of treatment with the effluent sent into the sea.

Electric power lines, connected to the regional system in Antalya, were extended throughout the area for a total of 38 km and the requisite substations constructed. Street lighting was installed in Kemer as part of its electrification. A plant for solid refuse disposal was constructed, with collection of refuse from the hotels and communities by compactor refuse trucks and disposal in a sanitary land fill. Telephone facilities and services were provided including construction of an underground cable network. In order to prevent flooding of some of the river areas, regulation and irrigation works were constructed.

The Kemer Yacht Marina, one of a chain of marinas on the Aegean and Mediterranean Coast, has a capacity for 150 boats of various sizes and includes land parking boat facilities. Associated with the marina are a boat maintenance yard, repair and storage facilities, a 1.5-km promenade, three restaurants, eight shops, a watch tower, administration building, open air cafes, sports facilities, and a five star, 288-room marina hotel. A hotel school and training hotel have been developed. The project included the development of a modern health centre, the only one in South Antalya, to serve residents and tourists. As part of the project, a building was constructed to serve the combined functions of

Figure 13

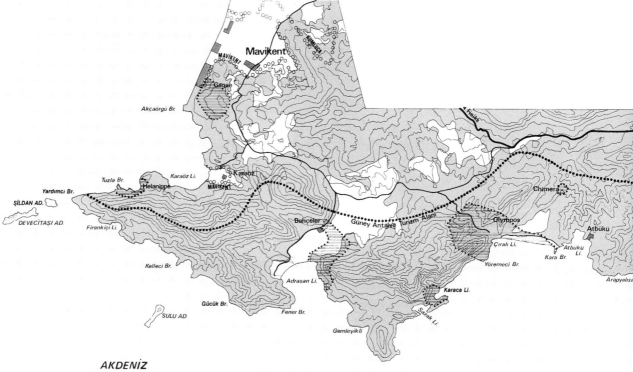

Figure 14

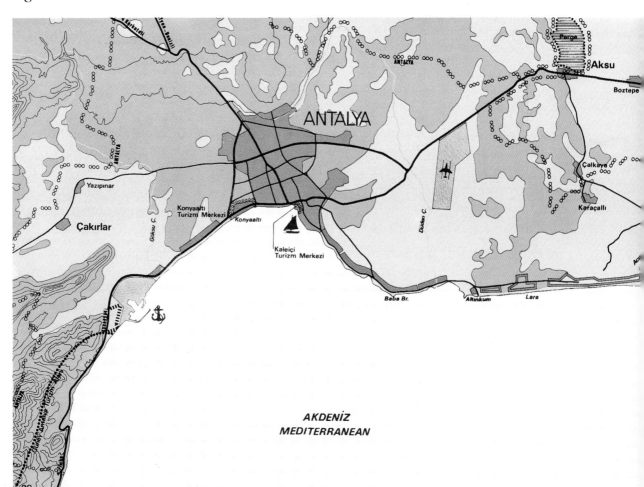

92

GÜNEY ANTALYA

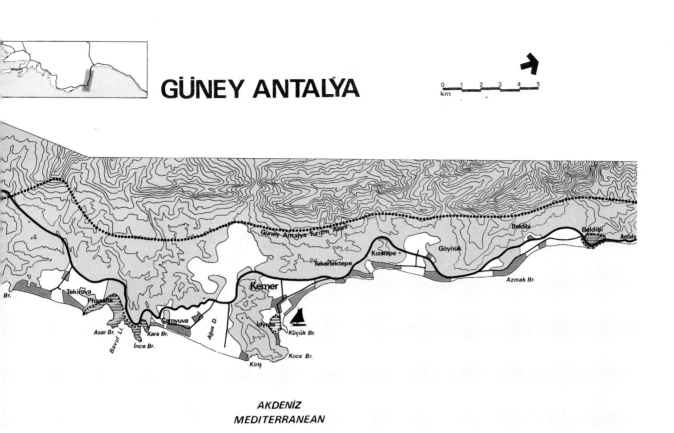

AKDENIZ
MEDITERRANEAN

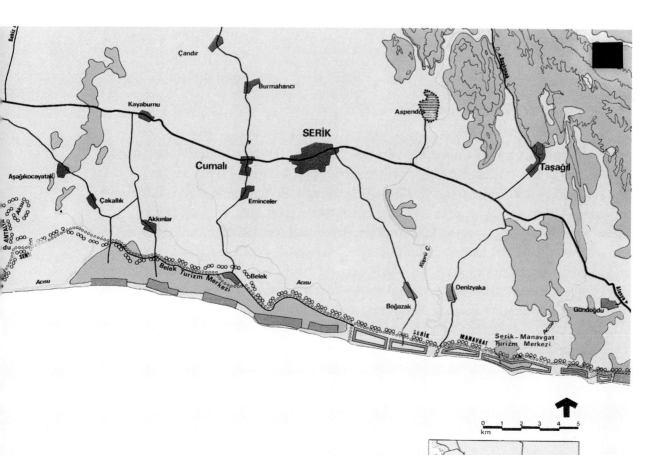

ANTALYA

municipality and tourism offices and the tourist information centre. As mentioned, fire fighting equipment and facilities were developed. Forest roads and fire watch towers and camping facilities including electricity were also developed. An exhibit building was constructed at the Phaselis ancient city ruins and provided with a water supply and electricity.

Housing was constructed in Kemer for some of the government and tourism employees involved in the project. This took the form of 16 apartment blocks with 126 flats of 65, 75 and 85 m2. In addition, an accommodation block for 150 single people and a nursery/primary school for 120 children were developed. Employees not living in this complex find private housing in Kemer and the villages. A middle school has also been constructed to serve the area.

Economic Impact Analysis

A detailed economic impact analysis is not available but, based on government estimates of the allocated accommodation, 20,000 jobs and foreign exchange earnings of more than US$450 mn have been generated. When South Antalya is fully developed, according to the plan, the benefits will be considerably greater. In addition, the residents of the region have benefited from improved infrastructure, medical and other services, substantial recreation facilities have been provided for local residents and Turks from elsewhere in the country, and the irrigation works have led to improvements in local agricultural output. Cultural and natural sites have also been conserved through the impetus of the project.

Regional Relationships

As has already been explained, tourism development has been highly integrated in the local communities within South Antalya, with Kemer serving as the tourism centre and service town. The other villages also provide some tourism services. Within the context of the entire Antalya region, Antalya city is the gateway to South Antalya and East Antalya, providing air and national highway access and substantial tourist attractions, facilities and services. Kemer is about 40 km away from Antalya on good roads, so that city is easily accessible to Kemer and its nearby accommodation sites. East of Antalya city, there are important sites such as the Roman city ruins at Perge and the Roman stadium at Aspendos.

At the national level, South Antalya was planned and functions as one of a network of tourism areas on the Aegean and Mediterranean Coast. It is well connected by air and road to the major cities of Istanbul and Ankara, which have their own important urban and tourist attractions. With respect to yachting tourism, the Kemer marina serves as one of the stopping points for yachts touring the coastal area of Turkey.

DEVELOPMENT IMPLEMENTATION

Organisation and Responsibilities for Implementation

As indicated in the initial agreement with the World Bank, the overall responsibility for the South Antalya project was given to the Ministry of Tourism, which appointed the Tourism Bank as the consultant company or functional executing entity. The Tourism Bank carried out the different activities required to implement the specific projects involved (with the approval of the Ministry of Tourism). These included issuing invitations to tender for the construction work, monitoring the construction, issuing the final acceptance of works, and managing the infrastructure where relevant. Some of the infrastructure work was undertaken by existing agencies and the developments are operated by them.

• The major highway and secondary roads were developed and are maintained by the Turkish State Highways Department.

• Development of the electric power network was carried out by Kepez AS, the public power utility company, and the electricity system is maintained by the same company.

• Development and operation of the telephone system is the responsibility of the Directorate of Post, Telegraph and Telephones (an international direct dialling facility is available).

• Electric power and service units at the Kindilcesme Camping Area were developed by the Directorate of National Parks.

• River flood control and agricultural irrigation works were implemented by the General Directorate of State Hydraulics.

• The Physelis ancient city exhibition and services buildings and related infrastructure were developed by the Ministry of Culture.

   The development and management of water supply, sewage and solid waste disposal and other project facilities and services were implemented by the Tourism Bank and are now carried out by local organisations within the project area that were established in the late-1980s. The South Antalya Tourism Infrastructure Management Organisation (SATIMO) was formed as the government policy making body. The executing management organisation is ALTAS (Altyapi Isletme ve Turizm AS), established by the municipality, which is 49 per cent owned by private sector companies (about 25 shareholders) and 51 per cent owned by SATIMO. ALTAS is financially self-sufficient through the collection of user fees for water supply, sewage and solid waste systems, as well as permit fees for development projects. It also manages, with government, the fire protection, health services and other operations. ALTAS has its own general director and staff, including a technical consultant, and shares an office building with the municipality administration in Kemer. ALTAS is the only resort infrastructure development and management agency of its kind so far in the country.

Once the development of hotels and the required infrastructure for the South Antalya project are completed, the Ministry of Tourism will be responsible for advertising, receiving and reviewing development proposals including planning and design concepts, development scheduling, financial arrangements and management structure, selecting the best overall proposal and giving permission for the private development to proceed.

One of the reasons for the successful planning and implementation of the project is attributed to the initial coordination in planning and development by central government. This was maintained through the involvement of ALTAS in carrying out the infrastructure development and management. At the time of the initial development, South Antalya had no municipal government, and the Ministry of Tourism and the Tourism Bank implemented the project. By the time the municipality was established and SATIMO and ALTAS were organised, the development pattern had been set and the necessary local management capabilities has been sufficiently developed to continue developing and managing the project.

The experience of projects elsewhere in the country has apparently not been as satisfactory as in Antalya. In 1985, physical planning, including tourism areas, was decentralised to municipal governments in the country — an approach that in concept was logical. However, the municipalities did not have any understanding of planning and the importance of adequate infrastructure development, or experience with systematic implementation techniques. This, along with the problems of development pressures being exerted on the local governments, has led to uncontrolled tourism development with inadequate infrastructure and rapid urban growth in some places. The programme now is to educate municipalities generally about the importance of planning and controlling development and to train their technical staff to plan and implement developments effectively. In order to avoid serious problems in tourism areas in the near future, the regulation was changed so that the central government now again maintains control of planning and development in the designated tourism areas.

In other tourism areas, which are increasing in number and size, the capability of developing all the required infrastructure for acceptable tourism development is lacking. So it has become necessary to slow the growth of tourism development in order for the proper infrastructure to be developed. In addition, a policy has been adopted to permit and encourage private sector development of infrastructure, such as marinas, airports and other components, leading up to more complete privatisation, but within the framework of government plans and development controls. An example of this approach is in the newly developing tourism area of East Antalya where private developers have formed an association that develops and manages the infrastructure, all with their own private capital. But the development will be based on tourism plans and development standards prepared by the Ministry of Tourism.

With respect to the development of commercial tourist facilities, the original national development approach was that the government would provide the infrastructure and the private sector would develop the superstructure of accommodation and other commercial tourist facilities. However, it was recognised that the government would need to be a pioneer in development, including the establishment of suitable development and design standards. This resulted in the creation of TURBAN, a state owned company for the development of hotels and other tourist facilities. This company developed some 23 hotels and holiday villages and six marinas in the country including the marina hotel in South Antalya. These were the best facilities then available for tourists. Since that earlier period of tourism development, it has become easier to attract private investment, and the TURBAN facilities are being privatised, with the company now functioning as a management organisation. The financing of private sector facility investment is now supported by the Development Bank of Turkey.

Land Acquisition and Development Programming

The major portion of the land required for development sites in the South Antalya project area was already owned by the government. The private parcels that had to be acquired, including land alongside the roads, were purchased at market value. Later, in the acquisition stage, the planning law was changed to provide for an exchange of private land. This means that when land is taken over for tourism use, alternative parcels of government land located elsewhere in the same general area are given in exchange. There was initially some opposition by local landowners to this acquisition of land for tourism. But once it was realised that it would bring substantial benefits in the form of improved infrastructure and public facilities, such as schools and medical services and employment in tourism, there was a change in attitude. Many meetings were held with villagers during this initial period of development.

Implementation of the project components was initially programmed to meet development schedules and targets. Much of the infrastructure and initial development within the area and some public facilities, including the health clinic, hotel school, fire fighting operations, were completed in the late 1970s and early 1980s. The Kemer Yacht Marina was opened in 1985, the associated TURBAN marina hotel in 1988 and training hotel in 1989. The housing community for employees was finished in 1987. The municipality/ALTAS office and information centre is completed. However, there was some difficulty in attracting private investment in hotels until greater incentives were offered in the early to mid-1980s.

Some of the other problems encountered in implementation, according to the government, were: difficulty in maintaining the desired density levels and enforcing some of the land use controls; the high migration of unskilled people from other parts of Turkey to Antalya looking for employment, with insufficient local housing and community facilities available for these migrants; and the challenge of coordinating all the various agencies and public utilities involved in the development (which lead to the creation of SATIMO and ALTAS). Since central government is responsible for planning and the regional and local governments are responsible for implementation, close coordination is required among the different government levels.

Current Status of Development and Planning

The status of infrastructure and public facility development was described in the previous section. By 1991, 58 sites had been allocated to private enterprises developing accommodation facilities (existing, under construction and approved) as follows:

Table 5: Current status of hotel development in South Antalya	
Type of Accommodation	Number of Beds
5-star hotels	5,244
4-star hotels	2,103
3-star hotels	1,485
2-star hotel	40
1-star hotels	146
First class holiday village	14,644
Pensions/guest houses	164
Camping areas	2,212
Total	26,038

Thus, in terms of bed capacity, the project is approaching 40 per cent of its intended full capacity. In addition, a day use recreation area with a capacity of 750 has been allocated, and the two 18-hole golf courses are underway. In line with the policy of encouraging small-scale accommodation, small hotels, guest houses and some self-catering units are being privately developed in Kemer and some of the villages. Shopping facilities, tour agencies and other tourist-oriented enterprises have also been developed in Kemer.

Expansion of the infrastructure progresses as the facility sites are allocated. The programme of ALTAS is to consolidate and centralise the sewage and water treatment plants for more efficient operation of those systems, and a loan may be taken out to finance this project. It would be repaid from future user fees. The present technique of using sanitary land fill for disposal of solid waste is not considered totally satisfactory, and plans are underway for improvements, possibly to dispose of organic matter in a treatment plant. Detailed plans are also being prepared for new development sites. Planning studies for the Adrasan site in the south are underway, as is the plan for a new tourism service area to provide more housing and community facilities for people working in tourism.

The leading tourist market for South Antalya is currently Germany, followed by Scandinavia and France. South Antalya has a higher quality tourism product image than some other resort destinations in Turkey. The Germans are also a major market for yachting tourism, and some keep their boats permanently based in the Kemer Yacht Marina. During the tourist season, occupancy rates are high in the hotels, often up to 90-95 per cent. However, seasonality is a problem in South Antalya, as well as in the country generally. Some of the hotels close during the low winter season.

In recognition of this problem, the 1990 revised plan for the area includes plans for a greater diversity of tourist attractions and facilities in order to broaden the tourist markets, increase the average length of stay, and attract more tourists during the low season. Priority is being given, for example, to development of the golf courses, entertainment centres and the proposed health centre. Riding and hiking are being encouraged in the mountain areas, and discounted rates are being offered during the low season, especially to attract domestic tourists.

Socio-Economic and Environmental Impact

Tourism has already brought considerable economic and social benefits to South Antalya and its citizens. Agricultural improvements resulting from the project's irrigation works have increased the local production of food items for which there is now a good market in the hotels and restaurants. Initially, there was some resistance to the purchase of local private property for tourism use, but this was overcome, as has been explained.

The attraction of unskilled migrants to Antalya from elsewhere in Turkey has generated some stress on local housing and community services which has not yet been completely resolved.

There does not seem to be any significant negative environmental impact resulting from the tourism development because of the careful planning of the project, the development of adequate infrastructure, and the application of development and design controls, such as regulations on the protection of trees. In fact, the development of the infrastructure has probably improved the environmental health standards of the residents. What has been especially important is the provision of an adequate water supply and sewage and solid waste disposal systems which, as already mentioned, are to be further improved in the near future. ALTAS has a programme for continuous spraying to control insects in the area.

Although not in the South Antalya project area, it is worthwhile noting the environmental study on turtle nesting in East Antalya, which is being carried out by the Ministry of Tourism. Based on field research of the turtle nesting areas on the beaches in East Antalya, as part of the tourism planning of that region, techniques are being devised to protect the turtles' nesting habits and passage of the hatched baby turtles into the sea. These techniques include shielding the nesting areas from lights (which distract the turtles), prohibiting heavy vehicles on the beach, and prohibiting tourists with lights on the beach during the nesting season. The potential conflict between turtle nesting and tourism is compounded by the fact that the turtle nesting season coincides with the peak tourist season.

More generally, Turkey has recently adopted an environmental protection law and an Under Secretary for the Environment has been appointed. An Environmental Impact Assessment (EIA) procedure is under review but not yet adopted (as of early-1991). This law and procedure give greater assurance that new development projects, including tourism development, will be environmentally planned and will not result in serious environmental problems.

FINANCING OF PLANNING AND DEVELOPMENT

The original planning of South Antalya was undertaken with some international financial and technical assistance. Since then, the planning has been carried by the Physical Planning Section of the General Directorate of Investments, Ministry of Tourism, located in Ankara. This section has a trained and experienced technical staff.

The World Bank loan (an IDA credit that provides for no interest and a long grace period for repayment of the capital) of about US$26 mn made in 1977 was used mostly for the foreign exchange component of the infrastructure development, notably for the water supply and sewage systems, and also for some other components such as archaeological conservation and fire fighting equipment. The central government (through the Ministry of Tourism and Tourism Bank), the Highways Department and various public utility companies involved, paid for the remaining cost of the infrastructure. The hotel school received some technical and financial assistance (for equipment) from the International Labour Organization (ILO). The World Bank also provided some technical assistance initially, especially for coastal engineering, financial analysis and other areas of expertise.

As already mentioned, there was initial difficulty in attracting private sector investments for the development of accommodation and other commercial facilities. In 1980, the government underwent a restructuring and there was a general shift in policy towards encouraging private sector development, albeit allowing for the government to provide investment incentives. A Foreign Investment Law was adopted allowing up to 100 per cent foreign investment in projects, or joint ventures with Turkish companies and development banks. The Tourism Encouragement Act was adopted in 1982 and became operational in 1983, and other related regulations were adopted to encourage investment in tourism 6/.

The tourism investment incentives include provision for such factors as: allocation of state land at low lease rent; special loans for capital and the initial cost of operations; various types of tax exemptions such as value added tax, corporate income tax, property tax, and customs duties normally applied to imported materials used in tourism (but not for more than 10 per cent of the total project cost); and other concessions.

An interesting aspect of this law is that tourism investors are treated as exporters with exporters' preferential rights. In addition, tourism establishments may employ up to 20 per cent foreigners within their total staff count. Project sites for development are made available on a 49-year lease period at a low rent. In the case of South Antalya, provision of the infrastructure is also an incentive, since it is recognised that the investor must pay a development permit fee and user fees for much of the infrastructure.

The Development Bank of Turkey is, by policy, very involved in making concessionary loans to developers of accommodation and other tourist facility projects 7/. This bank provides loans for projects approved by the Ministry of Tourism for up to 50 per cent of the property value at interest rates which are substantially lower than commercial rates. Previously, loans were granted an eight-year repayment period including a two-year grace period but since 1991, loans have had a ten-year repayment period including a four-year grace period. The loans can be applied to the expansion of existing development, as well as new projects, and can be applied to various types of accommodation and other tourist facilities including hotels, holiday villages, small-scale accommodation (through local commercial banks), marinas, large yachts used for commercial tourist activities, health tourism facilities, golf courses and club houses, and tour and travel agencies. Loans may also be granted for marketing and training programmes.

In South Antalya, the Development Bank has granted loans for projects totalling more than 12,000 tourist beds, or close to 50 per cent of the 26,000 beds so far allocated for development. The distribution by type of accommodation is shown in Table 6.

The International Finance Corporation (IFC - part of the World Bank) has also granted loans to two Turkish companies for the development of hotels in South Antalya. As previously mentioned, the state company of TURBAN developed the marina hotel in Kemer. There is some international financing in certain hotel projects and some applications for international financing of projects are pending (1991).

The government believes that, with the various incentives and loans available and the generally favourable tourism growth trends in the country, there will be no problem in attracting investors for the development of tourist facilities; and that an adequate amount of capital is available within the country which can be attracted to tourism.

Table 6: Bed capacity in South Antalya according to type of accommodation		
Type of accommodation	No. of enterprises	No. of beds
5-star hotels	6	3,345
4-star hotels	4	1,190
3-star hotels	1	74
2-star hotels	2	76
Holiday villages (first class)	9	7,378
Pensions/guest houses	9	266
Total	35	12,389

OVERALL EVALUATION AND CONCLUSIONS

Area Planning

The South Antalya tourism plan, which encompasses an 80-km long coastal area and is included in the Olympus Seashore National Park, provides for some 65,500 tourist beds (equivalent to more than 30,000 rooms). It has been targeted for high quality tourism markets, and particularly international leisure tourists. But its facilities also cater to domestic tourists. The plan has proved to be an appropriate one that provides a functional, attractive, and environmentally sensitive tourism product, integrated into the regional setting and existing communities.

Modifications of the original plan maintained the initial development concepts but called for an increase in the extent of development. The expansion was able to be absorbed because of the size of the area and its many beaches and extensive mountain hinterland. Besides increased accommodation, the revised 1990 plan also recommended additional tourist recreation facilities and activity areas, reflecting the need to expand and diversify visitor activities in order to extend the tourist season. It also reflects the current European market trend towards more activity oriented holidays.

Emphasis on planning and development focused on the regional integration of tourism, which could provide a multi-purpose infrastructure serving both tourism and the existing local communities. This included facilities and services

102

such as a medical clinic and schools, which were greatly needed for the residents' welfare. The town of Kemer was designated as the main service town for tourism in the region, providing housing and community facilities for employees in tourism, and is the site of a major marina, related hotels and other tourist facilities. Both Kemer town and other villages in the region have substantially benefited from infrastructure and community facility improvements accomplished as part of the project. Agricultural improvements were made through the construction of irrigation systems combined with river flood control.

One very important component of the infrastructure was the development of a hotel school and training hotel to provide the necessary skilled personnel to work in tourism. Key regional infrastructure components developed were the airport near Antalya city which is the gateway to the region and a good highway between the airport and the South Antalya project area, in order to provide comfortable and easy access for tourists to South Antalya.

The planning approach used, together with the subsequent application of development and design controls, has maintained the environmental quality of the area. This has helped avoid any serious environmental problems. The only social problem resulting from the project seems to be the influx of unskilled workers seeking employment, thereby placing stress on local housing and community services. More generally, Turkey has adopted an Environmental Protection Law and is preparing Environmental Impact Assessment standards and procedures to be applied to specific development projects.

South Antalya was planned within the context of national planning for tourism in Turkey which focuses on the coastal regions of the Aegean and Mediterranean Seas, as well as on some inland areas. The areas designated for tourism in the country are systematically undergoing development, reflecting the government's policy of giving high priority to tourism because of its economic and social benefits.

Development Implementation

The implementation approach involved planning and initial infrastructure and public facility financing (with World Bank assistance) and development by central government. The project was then taken over and managed by local entities. However, the central Ministry of Tourism still carries out the detailed planning needed and maintains control over the review and approval of private development proposals to ensure that the desired type of accommodation and other facility development is achieved. ALTAS, the local agency established to continue developing and managing the infrastructure in South Antalya and which has joint government and private sector ownership, has been an effective mechanism for infrastructure management.

Because of the inexperience of local government with tourism development in South Antalya, it has been seen that the central government still needs to retain a strong role in development planning and implementation. However, the private sector is responsible for development of accommodation and other commercial tourist facilities within the framework of central government plans and development controls. This approach has been an effective one overall.

The infrastructure development programme is now largely completed for the present level of development planned. The major initial difficulty encountered in implementation was attracting private sector investment for the development of accommodation and other tourist facilities. It was not until there was a major shift in general policy in the early 1980s and the adoption of tourism investment incentives in 1982 through the Tourism Encouragement Law and other regulations, that the private sector was induced to make investments. Since then development has taken place rapidly, with some 40 per cent of the accommodation bed capacity completed or scheduled for completion in the early-1990s. It is estimated that this level of development generates some 20,000 jobs locally and about US$450 mn of foreign exchange for the country.

An important role in private sector development financing is performed by the Development Bank of Turkey whose policy is to support tourism as well as other types of development. The Development Bank makes concessionary loans to private investors for all types of accommodation and other tourist facilities. A substantial proportion of the private tourism development in South Antalya and elsewhere in the country is being partially financed by this bank.

The South Antalya project is considered a model for integrated and controlled tourism development in Turkey and is hailed as its most successful large-scale tourism project. In addition to effective organisational approaches, the project benefited from adequate financing for the development of infrastructure and the continuing strict application of development and design controls. However, this financing is not automatically available to other tourism areas. An interesting approach being applied for development of tourism in East Antalya is the formation of an organisation of private investors and developers which will, from its own resources, develop and manage the required regional infrastructure with the individual private development of tourist facilities. However, tourism development will still take place within the framework of government planning and the application of development controls, in order to maintain the environmental quality of the area and bring benefits to local residents.

---

1. Ministry of Tourism (Turkey). *Bulletin of Tourism Statistics.* 1989, with some provisional data for 1990. These arrival figures include excursionists such as cruise ship passengers who do not stay overnight in onshore accommodation. The number of overnight tourists is somewhat lower than these figures.

2. Ministry of Tourism. *Turizm '89 - Tourism in Turkey.* 1990.

3. Department of Physical Planning and Projects, Tourism Bank. *Southwest Turkey Touristic Investment Areas.* December 1987.

4. Department of Planning, Ministry of Tourism. *South Antalya Tourism Development Plan.* 1990.

5. Ministry of Culture and Tourism/Tourism Bank. *Turizm Yatirim Alanlari — Kemer Imar Plani.* No date.

6. Ministry of Culture and Tourism. *Turkey - Tourism: Opportunities for Investors.* 1987, and T. C. Turizm Bankasi, A. S. *Legal and Financial Aspects of Tourism Investment in Turkey.* July 1988.

7. Development Bank of Turkey. *Principles and Conditions of Touristic Credits.* 1990.

Chapter 7

LANZAROTE TOURISM PLANNING PROJECT CANARY ISLANDS, SPAIN

The five preceding tourism projects concerned the development of new resorts. The objective of the Lanzarote project, on the other hand, was to control tourism in a mature resort, but one which is still expanding rapidly. Tourism had developed without any formal planning in Lanzarote until the moment when local citizens became concerned about its future relationship with the local community and especially the effects of tourism development on the aesthetic, environmental and socio-cultural setting of the island. This generated a series of technical studies and government hearings and resulted in ordinances which are referred to as the Insular Plan.

Tourism planning in Lanzarote is of special interest because of the tourism resources of the island, the identifiable relationship between tourism development and its effects on the supporting environment and society, and the formulation and adoption of the Insular Plan. Many of the approaches and planning techniques used to address major issues in this plan provide valuable lessons for those formulating or modifying tourism plans for mature and expanding resort areas elsewhere.

BACKGROUND

The Lanzarote Setting

Lanzarote is one of the seven major Canary Islands which form a Spanish territory lying in the Atlantic Ocean near the northwest coast of Africa. As shown in Figure 15, Lanzarote is located about 96-km west of Africa and 960-km southwest of the Spanish mainland. It is the most northeasterly of the seven sister islands.

Lanzarote is a volcanic island but one which is relatively flat, with the highest elevation being only 670-m. This low terrain means it has very little rain and the climate is quite dry. The average annual rainfall is only 140-mm, and the island suffers from chronic shortages of fresh water. A public desalinisation plant is a major source of drinking water on the island. The climate is also temperate. Weather is pleasant year round, although the winters are somewhat cool. The average annual temperature is 20°C (68°F). The climate is affected by the continuous trade winds as well as by the adjacent Gulf Stream which moderate the desert heat of the nearby Sahara.

Figure 15

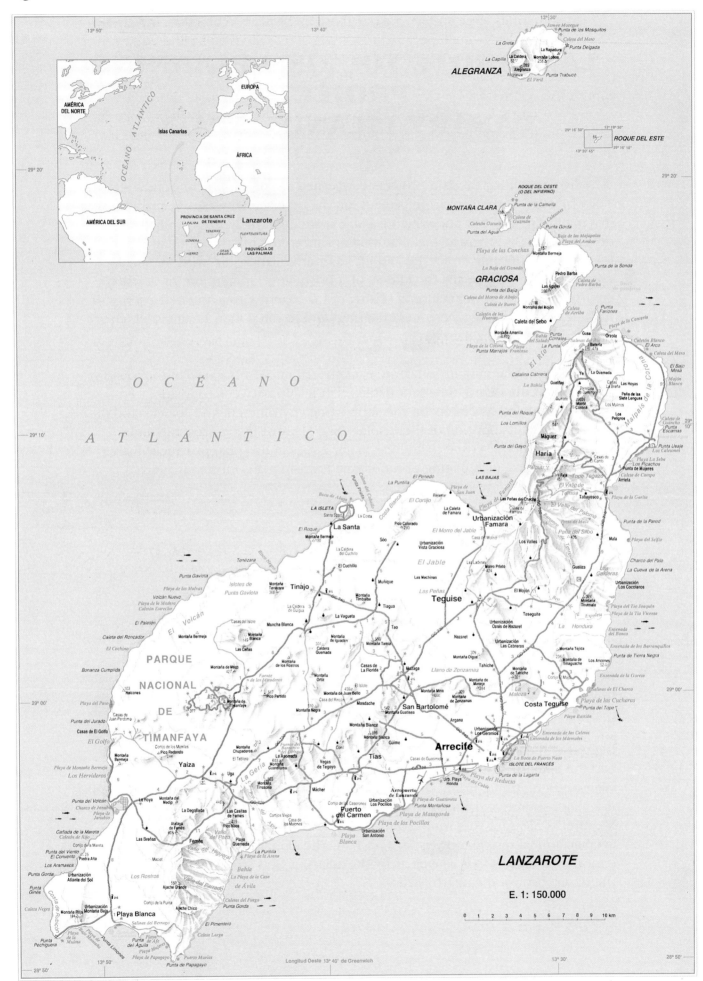

LANZAROTE

E. 1: 150.000

0 1 2 3 4 5 6 7 8 9 10 km

In spite of its large surface area of about 800 square kilometers, Lanzarote has historically had a small population. This is due to the island's limited supply of water and other natural resources necessary to support population growth. Local authorities estimate that the current population is 80,000, of which approximately 20,000 are recent immigrants. The principal industries were fishing and subsistence farming until the tourism sector began to flourish in the mid-1970s. Today, public officials estimate that over 75 per cent of employment in Lanzarote can be attributed directly or indirectly to tourism.

The Canary Islands have a regional government located in Tenerife. On Lanzarote, there is a subordinate island government (the Cabildo) as well as seven district (municipal) governments.

Tourist Attractions on Lanzarote

Like many island destinations, the main tourist attractions of Lanzarote are its warm and sunny climate and beaches. However, the island also possesses several natural and cultural attractions, of which the principal ones are:

• General scenic beauty and natural geographic attractions of the island.

• Artistic character that pervades much of the local development and life-style.

• Distinctive features of the life-style of Lanzaroteans.

• Various scenic and natural sites that have been developed for visitor use.

The general scenic beauty and natural attractions include a variety of striking volcanic land forms, a marine nature preserve, interesting tidal water features, numerous coves and broad beaches, and offshore islands.

The artistic traditions and character of Lanzaroteans are evident in many aspects of traditional development on the island. The architecture, with its distinctive white masonry walls and green or blue trim, is simple and attractive. This style prevails in hotels as well as residences. Many of the historic buildings have been well preserved and several new monuments have been built. In addition, there is an expanding landscaping campaign to enhance roadsides and public areas. A major proponent of these endeavours is the local artist, Cesar Manrique, who also has designed several of the tourist facilities on the island.

The farming techniques used on Lanzarote are of great interest to tourists. Large areas of the landscape are interspersed with interesting half-moon stone conical formations. These unusual earthworks, which are based on techniques developed centuries ago, capture scarce precipitation for the growing of crops. Cultural attractions include several fortresses and other colonial buildings, traditional fishing villages, museums, traditional dress, dance, arts, crafts, and sports. The hospitality of Lanzaroteans is also an important tourist attraction.

A review of the major natural attractions that have been imaginatively developed for visitor use indicates the creative approach being taken towards tourism on Lanzarote. These features, developed with such facilities as access roads and walkways, exhibits, restaurants, souvenir shops and parking areas, include:

- Jameos del Agua — This attraction is part of the longest volcanic tunnel in the world. It has two large sections, the first a water-filled grotto containing a rare albino crab and the second, containing a large performing arts auditorium. Facilities include an 'al fresco' restaurant and souvenir shop. The overall design of facilities is one of the most interesting features.

- Mirador del Rio — This structure is built on a steep cliff overlooking the striking vistas of the northern shore of Lanzarote and the nearby small island of La Graciosa. It is constructed on the site of a former coastal fortification and is also unique in design.

- Cueva de los Verdes (Green Caves) — These spacious caves are an extension of the volcanic tunnel that forms Jameos del Agua. Tours of the caves have to be conducted by special guides because of the dangers posed by their many turns and a deep abyss.

- Montañas del Fuego (Fire Mountains) — The main attraction is a tourist centre located in the Timanfaya National Park, which encompasses many of the lava flows from the last major eruption on Lanzarote. Tours of the remarkable volcanic terrain can be taken by bus or camel. A mountain-top restaurant features food cooked using the volcanic heat from a chasm and geysers, and fires started from the ground heat.

- Jardin de Cactus (Cactus Garden) — This botanical garden features many species of cacti. It was developed in an abandoned quarry and its intricate stonework and stunning earthen columns make it a work of art as well as a garden.

It is not only the existence of these attractions, but also the high standard of their preservation and presentation that differentiates Lanzarote from other beach resorts. Facilities have been designed to preserve the character of the natural features, and are very artistically developed and well maintained. As a result, tourists take particular care to avoid causing any damage.

The sites are visited by both tourists and local residents, many of whom attend special events held at the attractions and use the restaurant facilities. The number of visitors for these attractions has been increasing over the past several years, totalling over 1.6 mn in 1990 for the five major sites. However, although these attractions are important to tourism development in the islands, they are also rather fragile and could lose their appeal if tourism development expands in an uncontrolled manner.

Tourism Growth on Lanzarote

Tourism on Lanzarote was of minor importance until European tour operators began aggressively promoting the island in the mid-1970s. As indicated in Table 7, most of the growth in tourism occurred during the past decade. This expansion was fuelled mainly by charter flights and package tours from Germany and the UK. Estimates suggest that more than 80 per cent of visitors in 1990 were on inclusive package tours (ITs).

Secondary sources include the Spanish mainland, Finland, Sweden and Norway. Yet the growth in tourism has not been consistent on a year by year basis. The slowing economy, warm winter in Europe and the appreciation of the peso resulted in a stagnation of tourist arrivals in 1989. But they picked up sharply in 1990.

There is some seasonality of tourism in Lanzarote. Winter is the peak season, providing an escape for many northern Europeans from the cold European winters. Most of the recent marketing efforts of hotels and the Lanzarote Tourism Promotion Board have been focused on the mainland Spanish market because Spaniards tend to visit the island outside the peak winter season.

Table 7:

Growth in tourist arrivals in Lanzarote, 1971-90

| Origin | No. of tourist arrivals in Lanzarote | | |
	1971	1980	1990
Germany	9,707	65,085	251,957
UK	3,448	33,676	237,619
Spain	...	...	113,182
Finland	...	...	56,901
Sweden	...	...	46,781
Norway	...	...	43,672
Others	9,688	39,021	127,006
Total	22,843	137,782	877,118

available: ... = not

Current Status of Tourism Development

Tourism has developed in three main geographic regions — at Puerto del Carmen, Costa Teguise and Playa Blanca. All these regions are located in the southeastern part of Lanzarote, near Arrecife, the capital and only urban area on the island. Each tourism zone has excellent beaches and generally calm ocean waters.

The main concentration of tourist development is at Puerto del Carmen, which is reported to account for almost 70 per cent of all tourists visiting Lanzarote. The major attractions of this former fishing village are its expansive golden beaches and the charm of its still existent fishing harbour. Despite the considerable development that has taken place here, the beaches have remained clean and unpolluted. Most of the tourism development is low-rise, so development is spread over a fairly wide area. Most buildings have been built in the prevalent local architectural style.

Costa Teguise is a large, privately owned resort complex. The original 11,000 square meters of development land was purchased from local landowners by a Spanish company almost two decades ago. The resort was planned and developed along the shoreline, and included a desalination plant and the only 18-hole golf course on Lanzarote. The resort has many elements of a planned resort, including landscaped areas, an orderly street network, and centralised recreation centres. Accommodation at Costa Teguise includes a few four and five star, mid-rise (four to seven stories) hotels, but most of the existing development is in apartment complexes built in the traditional local style. Many individual apartments have been put on the market for sale to individual owners. There is also extensive development of commercial retail centres, and an excess supply of commercial space as is seen by the many unoccupied shops. It seems likely that the development of commercial space and the sale of apartments were attempts to recover the heavy initial investments required. Only a portion of the total resort is now developed and there is much land available for the additional development planned. The Spanish company that owned Costa Teguise was recently acquired by the Kuwaiti Investment Office.

Playa Blanca is a small resort with oceanfront promenades and harbours that maintain the character of its former role as a fishing village. Playa Blanca is the most remote of the three tourism zones, approximately 35-km from Arrecife. The beach areas of this resort are somewhat small, which limits the amount of development that can take place in the future.

Tourism officials indicate that there are approximately 25,000 tourist accommodation units on Lanzarote (equivalent to 50,000-60,000 tourist beds). The bulk of these units are apartments and there are fewer than 5,000 hotel rooms on the island.

Organisation of Tourism

The regional government of the Canary Islands has a Department of Tourism in the capital of Tenerife and various functions are delegated to the island government of Lanzarote, the Cabildo. In addition, a marketing organisation, the Lanzarote Tourist Promotion Board, was formed by the Cabildo to promote the island.

Tourism Education and Training

There are two government-operated educational establishments devoted to tourism in Lanzarote. One provides a range of university level courses, including four year degree courses in tourism management. The other is a vocational school that concentrates on the training of service employees. Its programmes are also up to four years long. The rapid expansion of tourism in recent years has somewhat strained the resources of these two facilities. There are not many local Lanzaroteans in executive positions in hotels on the island but their numbers are increasing.

Agriculture and Tourism

The relationship of agriculture and tourism in Lanzarote is complex. One clear impact of the expansion of tourism was a movement of labour from the lower paying agricultural sector to the tourism sector, resulting in declining land devoted to farming. This movement was not severe, because farms are generally small and do not require large numbers of full-time labourers. Many tourism employees live on family farms and occasionally help during harvest and other peak work periods.

Infrastructure and Housing

The infrastructure on Lanzarote is generally well developed. The international airport, while equipped only with basic facilities, is sufficiently large to handle current levels of traffic. The road network is extensive and highways are generally in good condition. Electric power, telephone and sewage services in populated areas are adequate.

The one major infrastructure problem in Lanzarote is water supply for both potable use and agricultural irrigation. There is insufficient ground water and, despite the spread of rainwater catchment techniques and innovative farming methods, the existing desalination plants are scarcely able to meet current levels of demand. The additional potable water required by more tourism development could only be provided by the construction of more desalination capacity. It is interesting to note that a major tourism project, Costa Teguise, did fund the development of a desalination plant, which also provides potable water for the local community.

In general, tourism development seems to have raised the level of infrastructure services on Lanzarote. However, the costs of developing this infrastructure are very high. In a recent article, it was estimated that the development of each new tourist bed on Lanzarote required a public investment of Pta 950,000 (US$10,200 at current exchange rates), of which US$8,600 was for infrastructure. In addition, the operating costs necessary to maintain the infrastructure have risen greatly. Tourism clearly helps to pay for both the development and maintenance of this infrastructure through user fees, the wages earned by tourism employees and the other benefits of a thriving economy. But it is not clear whether the tourism sector is paying its fair share.

Many Lanzaroteans believe that additional water supply and other infrastructure will be much more expensive in the future and that the price of water and public services will rise, which will make traditional farming even less economically viable.

The recent rapid growth of tourism and the influx of labour seem to have created some shortages in the housing supply. But the additional development of housing in recent years is easing the strain. The stock of housing on Lanzarote is expanding from two major sources: new development on family-owned lands and the development of apartments in resort areas. The pattern of land ownership on Lanzarote is characterised by numerous small farms and individual parcels, many of which have been owned by families for generations. There is much development of larger and new residences on these lands because of the land costs and the economic cost of construction using traditional methods. Some local residents also live in the resort area apartments.

While the current housing situation appears to be manageable, a high level of additional tourism development might require more extensive development of housing especially oriented to immigrant employees.

THE INSULAR PLAN

Impetus for the Plan

As tourism on Lanzarote expanded, the only significant control was exercised through the construction permit process of the seven municipalities. There were no formal written policies nor general plans which affected tourism development.

Tourism development was generally welcomed by Lanzaroteans as a means of improving a vulnerable economy until approximately 1986. By then, several factors had combined to cause concern among many residents. These factors included:

• The accelerated growth of tourism, from 177,193 tourists in 1983 to 414,733 tourists in 1986.

• The increasing density of development at Puerto del Carmen and Playa Blanca.

• Ambitious development plans at Costa Teguise which would have led to a resort several times larger than the one currently in existence.

112

• The growing demand for employment which could not be satisfied by local residents and was, therefore, causing increased in-migration.

• Shifts in employment from traditional agriculture and fishing to tourism, which may have contributed to the declining cultivation of traditional crops.

• Emerging environmental problems such as the adverse visual impact of development, excessive mining of local cinder, and selective deterioration of the island's aquifer.

• Skyrocketing municipal budgets, due in part to expenditure on infrastructure to support tourism.

Fortunately, the environmental and social impacts of tourism development were (and still are) limited. But there was considerable concern that future development could lead to major problems. This was vividly portrayed in supporting studies for the plan which analysed the potential development under three scenarios: a ceiling on development; controlled growth; and uncontrolled growth.

Table 8:

Accommodation development scenario for Lanzarote

Number of Tourist Beds Scenario	1991	1995	1999
Growth Ceiling	53,300	60,000	60,000
Controlled Growth	60,000	80,000	90,000
Uncontrolled Growth	74,600	130,600	191,200

According to this study, the demand for tourism under the uncontrolled growth scenario would have required enormous increases in the supply of accommodation on Lanzarote. The consequences of development of the magnitude forecast in the uncontrolled growth scenario would have included a sharply expanding imbalance between the existing population and the demand for labour and increasing demands on limited infrastructure. Moreover, the study concluded that uncontrolled growth might lead to severe deterioration of the environmental quality and socio-cultural character of Lanzarote, as indicated in *Figure 16.*

Figure 16

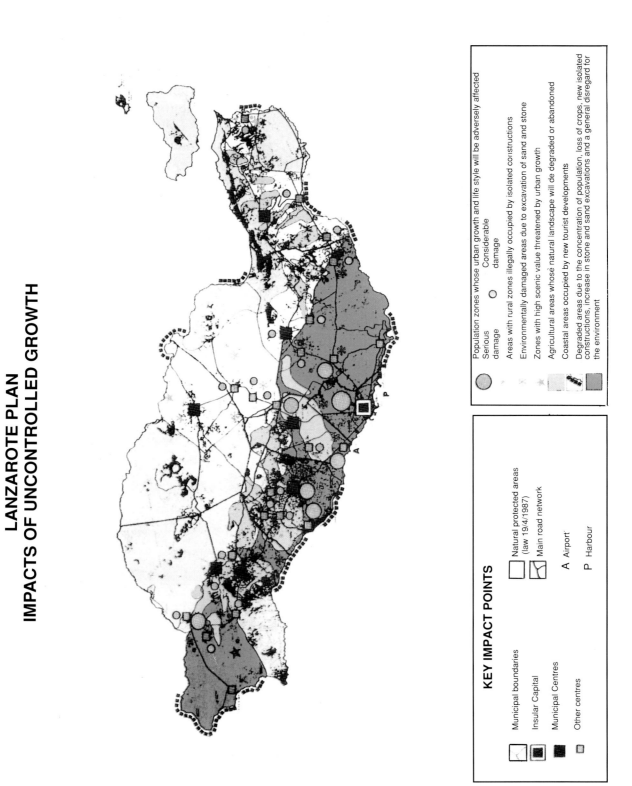

**LANZAROTE PLAN
IMPACTS OF UNCONTROLLED GROWTH**

KEY IMPACT POINTS

Municipal boundaries

Insular Capital

Municipal Centres

Other centres

Natural protected areas (law 19/4/1987)

Main road network

A Airport

P Harbour

Population zones whose urban growth and life style will be adversely affected

Serious damage   Considerable damage

Areas with rural zones illegally occupied by isolated constructions

Environmentally damaged areas due to excavation of sand and stone

Zones with high scenic value threatened by urban growth

Agricultural areas whose natural landscape will de degraded or abandoned

Coastal areas occupied by new tourist developments

Degraded areas due to the concentration of population, loss of crops, new isolated constructions, increase in stone and sand excavations and a general disregard for the environment

Evolution of the Plan

As already indicated, the island government, the Cabildo, started its analysis of all developments on Lanzarote, and notably tourism developments, in 1986. It was decided to prepare an Insular Plan, which would address land uses on the entire island as well as economic, environmental and socio-cultural aspects of development. (The Insular Plan is similar to what is usually termed a general or comprehensive plan.) In order to forestall the accelerated submission of building permits that was likely to occur, the Cabildo declared a moratorium on new development approvals in 1987.

A multi-disciplinary consulting team was assembled to study the long term development of Lanzarote and assist in the formulation of a draft Insular Plan. After the draft was prepared, it was then presented and reviewed in a series of three major public hearings organised by the Cabildo in 1987, 1989 and 1990. The plan was modified many times and was subject to some conflicting pressures from the seven municipalities, each of which had to give its endorsement. In spite of the intricacies of this political process, this approach resulted in a plan that was overwhelmingly endorsed by almost all the residents of Lanzarote and formally adopted by the Cabildo in 1990. The last step, which was the ratification of the Insular Plan by the regional government of the Canaries in Tenerife, was due to take place in early 1991.

Objectives and Concept of the Plan

The purpose of the Insular Plan was to control tourism development in such a way as to optimise its benefits without damaging the natural assets and socio-cultural patterns of Lanzarote. The basic objectives of the plan were to achieve:

- Balanced economic development that respects the island's unique geography and preserves the integrity of its environment.

- Correction of any existing environmental and socio-cultural problems, the strengthening of traditional life styles, and the prevention of any future adverse impact.

- Balanced urbanisation that minimises social costs.

- Planning of support facilities in sufficient quantity and spread throughout the island.

- Tourism development that takes into account the capacity of existing infrastructure and the cost of additional infrastructure.

- Conservation and revitalisation of the towns and architecture of Lanzarote.

- Implementation of the new development plan with due consideration for current development forces, thereby minimising major disruptions to the economy and society.

The Insular Plan was prepared according to these objectives. It was funded jointly by the regional government of the Canary Islands and the Cabildo (which also receives most of its funds from the regional government). The plan ultimately took the form of regulations, land use maps, and other guidelines contained in ordinances enacted by the Cabildo. The jurisdiction of the plan extended to the whole of Lanzarote. The land use and tourism structure plans are presented, respectively, in *Figures 17 and 18*.

A principal result of the plan is a limitation on development — the plan permitted the development of no more than 80,000 tourist beds by the year 2000. The location of development was also controlled as building was prohibited on almost 90 per cent of the island. In addition, the density of development permitted was reduced in a variety of ways. As an example, the plan mandated a height limitation of three stories and called for extended setbacks from the shoreline for tourist facilities.

The standard of development was addressed in the plan. In general, the various regulations require that subsequent development be of a higher quality than that allowed previously. In addition, new tourism development is required to adhere to the traditional architectural style of Lanzarote.

Market Issues

The proponents of the Insular Plan cited several market problems that could be partially remedied if the growth of tourism was controlled. These included the existing poorly diversified market, the high proportion of apartments, and the need for a higher standard of clientele.

Approximately 56 per cent of foreign tourists to Lanzarote were from the UK and Germany in 1990. This unhealthy dependence on only two markets alarmed Lanzaroteans who feared that problems in one or both of those countries could greatly upset tourism on the island. One desired result of controlled growth could be a more diversified and therefore less vulnerable market mix. The high proportion of tourist apartments on Lanzarote was also causing concern. Apartments require much more land than hotels, and tourists who stay in apartments generally spend less on a daily basis. One way to increase economic benefits and reduce unit infrastructure costs might be to encourage a higher proportion of hotels rather than apartment units.

As already indicated, most of the tourists coming to Lanzarote arrive on charter flights and/or package tours. This type of market is fairly low yield, since rooms and tourist services are offered at fairly heavily discounted rates. If demand continues to grow and the supply of accommodation is limited, the natural result would be upward pressure on the prices of tourist facilities and services. Thus, the economic benefits to Lanzarote could continue to increase without large investment in new infrastructure and new accommodation. However, any big increase in rates for price sensitive package tourists may have a negative impact on demand.

Figure 17

LANZAROTE LAND USE STRUCTURE PLAN

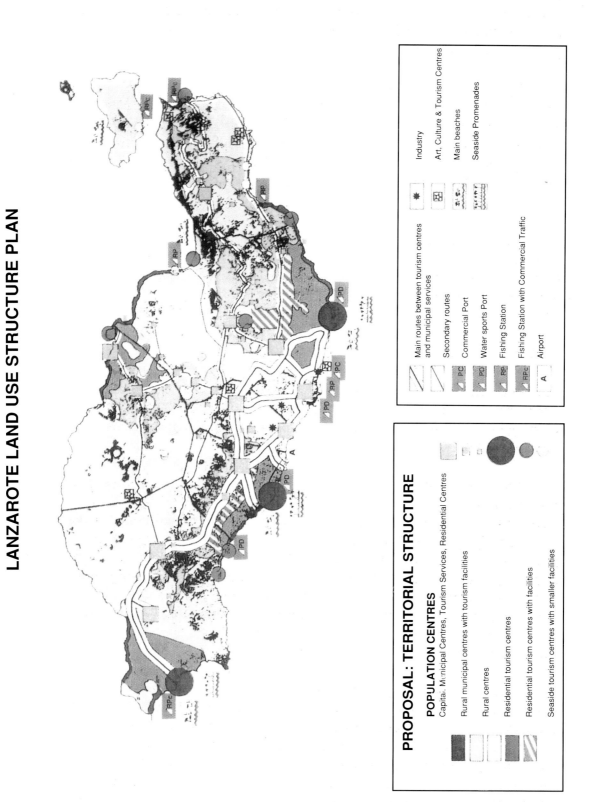

PROPOSAL: TERRITORIAL STRUCTURE

POPULATION CENTRES

Capital, Municipal Centres, Tourism Services, Residential Centres

Rural municipal centres with tourism facilities

Rural centres

Residential tourism centres

Residential tourism centres with facilities

Seaside tourism centres with smaller facilities

Main routes between tourism centres and municipal services

Secondary routes

PC — Commercial Port

PD — Water sports Port

RP — Fishing Station

RPc — Fishing Station with Commercial Traffic

A — Airport

Industry

Art, Culture & Tourism Centres

Main beaches

Seaside Promenades

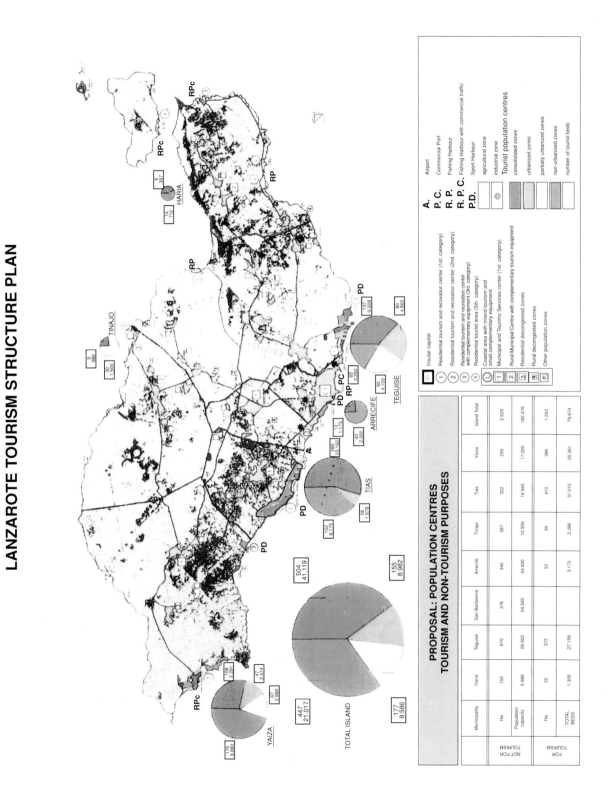

Figure 18

The Lanzarote coast, Lanzarote, Canaries Islands

Overall view of the Lanzarote urban area

Playa el Papagayo, a popular Lanzarote beach site

The Montañas del Fuego, an ancient volcanic area that was visited by over one-half million visitors in 1990

A view of the cultivated landscape using the distinctive farming techniques employed in Lanzarote

Aeriel view of Lanzarote and the resort development area

Socio-Economic and Environmental Considerations

Tourism is the major contributor to Lanzarote's economy, providing direct and indirect employment for as much as 75 per cent of the labour force, according to tourism officials. The outlook of other sectors is decidedly poor. The fishing industry is in decline after the territorial waters of the Canaries were reduced in a dispute with some African countries, and only small quantities of three cultivated products — onions, sweet potatoes and the cochineal beetle — are exported.

Tourism in Lanzarote has clearly provided a great number of economic benefits of the type normally derived from a healthy economy, and it has done so in a place where there are few, if any, viable economic alternatives. Nevertheless, it is evident that most Lanzaroteans doubt the benefits of a continued rapid expansion of the tourism sector. Many view the prospect of any further growth with concern, believing it would generate excessive in-migration, increased urbanisation, environmental disturbances, socio-cultural problems, and other harmful effects. In addition, it seems to be widely agreed that any erosion of the quality of tourism resources would render Lanzarote less attractive as a tourist destination, thereby leading to reductions in that economic activity.

Lanzaroteans are also worried that too much tourism development will cause farming and fishing to decline further. Most residents are proud of their special heritage and wish to retain the traditional practices involved in these activities. Such a decline could also have economic consequences in that the economy would be less diversified. So problems in the tourism sector would have even more severe economic effects on Lanzarote. In addition, the absence of farming and fishing, which are in themselves tourist attractions, would make Lanzarote less appealing to tourists.

The three geographic concentrations of tourism on Lanzarote are each in separate municipalities, and these have considerably larger public budgets than municipalities without much tourism. For example, the budget for the municipality of Tinajo (which has limited tourism) was less than 10 per cent of the equivalent budget for the tourist region of Yaiza, in spite of Tinajo's much larger population. In the course of the preparation of the Insular Plan, considerable resentment surfaced from among the municipalities that receive fewer funds. A reduction in spending for the development of infrastructure in tourism districts was viewed by many as a means of redirecting larger shares of public monies to the municipalities that had been receiving less funding.

Implementation of the Plan

The municipalities are responsible for approving applications for tourism developments within their boundaries. However, any development authorised by the municipalities must conform to the Insular Plan, which is superior to any municipal plans. The active involvement of the citizens of Lanzarote in the formulation of the Insular Plan would indicate that their participation is likely to continue in the implementation process, especially in the review and approval procedure of development projects by municipal authorities.

As indicated, it is expected that the Insular Plan will be enacted by the Canary Islands government in 1991. Because of the infancy of the plan, the effectiveness of its implementation cannot yet be evaluated. However, the planning process appears to have been very useful in identifying and publicising major issues of tourism development and developing a consensus among Lanzaroteans about the type and extent of tourism desired on the island. With this broad public support, the prospects for plan implementation seem quite optimistic.

OVERALL EVALUATION AND CONCLUSIONS

Form of the Insular Plan

The Insular Plan of Lanzarote is a general plan that is concerned not only with economic but also environmental and socio-cultural issues, and it is regional in scope. Moreover, it is inter-sectoral and therefore addresses all the economic sectors and land use patterns including tourism. This comprehensive approach is extremely valuable in integrating tourism development objectives and recommendations for future growth into the total development goals and patterns of the island, and in taking account of all the types of growth issues affecting the economy, society and environment.

In Lanzarote, tourism became the focus of this general plan because it is the dominant economic activity. As the engine for economic growth on the island, tourism was planned so that it would provide the types of benefits desired by the general public. The Insular Plan appears to contain reasonable targets and limits for tourism growth and prudent guidelines for improving the quality of tourism development. It does not specifically present policies for tourism, but it certainly establishes strong bases for them.

The regional scope of the plan, encompassing the entire island, is logical because it comprises a natural geographic, as well as social, unit and is isolated. In this respect, Lanzarote is fortunate in that its society is cohesive and identifiable. In many regional planning situations, the inter-relationships between various groups of residents, their countrymen elsewhere and tourists are more complicated.

As a general plan, however, the Insular Plan does not contain the additional refinements of a tourism development plan, which would be the next logical step in the tourism planning process. A tourism development plan would contain more detailed analyses of tourist markets, attractions, accommodation, the economic, environmental and socio-cultural impact of tourism. It would also suggest ways to enhance the benefits and include specific policies and land use recommendations, and the institutional elements necessary for guiding tourism development.

Aspects of the Planning Process

The process involved in the formulation of the Insular Plan of Lanzarote produced a number of interesting findings, the most important of which were as follows:

120

- The most significant forces affecting the planning recommendations were related to the island's environment and life styles.

- Regional issues superseded local concerns in the planning process. Tourism projects were being approved by municipal authorities because of their local benefits, but the regional effects of this development took precedence in the planning process.

- There was considerable public input into the planning process, which apparently helped to clarify and refine the plan and certainly enhanced its acceptance on the island.

The planning process and its use of scenarios proved to be an excellent means of assessing the effects of tourism and economic development on Lanzarote and, through public participation, arriving at a consensus as to the direction and the general form of the desired future development structure of the environment, economy and society.

Implementation of the Plan

As already indicated, the guidelines for tourism development established by the Insular Plan are somewhat general. Much of their implementation is left to municipal authorities and are subject to interpretation. It is still too early to assess whether this flexibility will affect implementation of the plan and it is essential that local considerations in decision-making do not override the regional integrity of the plan. However, the participation of the public in the formulation of the plan and presumably, their continued involvement in its ongoing implementation, should help ensure that the plan is followed.

Application of the Lanzarote Planning Approach

It is axiomatic that the true test of the effectiveness of a tourism plan and its implementation is the actual development that results from it. Since the Insular Plan of Lanzarote has only recently been completed and yet to be implemented, a comprehensive evaluation of the plan is premature. Nevertheless, it is already clear that there are some aspects of the plan and its evolution which can be applied to the planning required in some other tourism areas. The basic conditions that influenced the Insular Plan are not dissimilar from those in many other mature tourist destinations throughout the world, despite the distinct character of Lanzarote's environment, economy and society. Some of these common conditions include the following:

- The rapid growth of tourism.

- Inadequate infrastructure to accommodate future growth.

- In-migration of people to satisfy expanding employment needs in tourism.

• Actual or potential adverse environmental impact from tourism growth.

• Changing socio-cultural patterns resulting from tourism.

The approaches and techniques used in Lanzarote to influence these forces and achieve highly controlled tourism development can provide useful guidance in the formulation of tourism plans in other regions that have significant existing tourism development. This approach could be even further refined with respect to the planning process, including more detailed analyses and more specific policies and recommendations, in order to achieve a substantive guide for future controlled growth.

---

1. Prats, Fernando and and Felipe Manchon. "Reflexiones Sobre Turismo, Territorio y Sociedad Desde el Plan Insular de Lanzarote." *Ciudad y Territorio.* July-September, 1988.

Chapter 8

GENERAL CONCLUSIONS

A number of general conclusions can be drawn from the case study evaluations and analyses. All the case studies demonstrate, albeit with varying degrees of success, that integrated resorts and resort areas can be very successful in generating the desired economic benefits of tourism, while minimising the environmental, socio-cultural and economic problems of development. But this depends on proper planning, implementation and management.

It should also be emphasised that these case studies were for resort areas in countries that did not have previous experience in developing integrated resorts. Therefore, the successful implementation of these resorts posed new challenges in organisation and financing that some other more mature tourism destinations, such as Hawaii and the French Riviera, have already faced.

General conclusions can be grouped under the headings of planning, implementation and management, and financial considerations. It must be recognised that while there are certain basic conclusions applicable to all new resort development, the situation in each tourism area is different. Some approaches that are effective in one country or region may be — but are not necessarily — transferable to other areas. Approaches must, in any event, be adapted to the prevailing conditions of the resort area and its country and region.

PLANNING

Easy access

One of the most basic of all planning considerations is that adequate access must be provided to new resorts — their country and region — from the major tourist market sources, whether international or domestic. This access can be by air, road and even water or rail, depending on the location of the targeted market sources. In many cases, this may require a change of transportation, such as from an international airport to a regional airport and then by road to the resort. But transfers should be kept to a minimum and effected as conveniently as possible to attract tourists.

Within the regional and national context

The resort should be planned within the regional and national context of the country's overall tourism development policy and physical structure, including location of other resort areas and relationships to major tourist attractions and activities. The best approach is to start by preparing a comprehensive national and regional tourism plan which identifies the resort being developed. At the local level, the resort should be planned with consideration given to its relationship to local communities, potential tourist attractions and infrastructure.

Site selection

The site of the resort should be determined according to a number of criteria, including: suitability for the type and size of resort planned and distance from potential tourist attractions; availability of land not required for more important uses or of high conservation value; easy accessibility; availability of, or feasibility of developing, an adequate infrastructure; and availability of the required amount of land, or feasibility of acquiring the land, without unduly disrupting existing settlement patterns. Undeveloped sites are clearly preferable.

Transportation network

The resort site and area should be carefully planned with respect to land use and circulation patterns. Whatever the type of resort, an efficient internal transportation system, incorporating public transport and footpaths, is especially important. Planning should be related to environmental analysis, market and economic analyses, and socio-cultural considerations where relevant, as well as sound planning principles. Public access should be incorporated into the resort plan. In areas with existing settlements, there should be local community participation in the planning process. Resort planning is a specialised field and experienced professionals should be employed to carry out the planning and related market and economic feasibility analyses.

Feasibility analyses

At both the national, regional and resort development levels, careful and realistic market and financial feasibility analyses should be conducted to ensure that the proposed resort will be economically viable, and to help determine the size and type of resort to be planned.

The resort plan, in both outline and final form, should be evaluated for its economic, environmental and socio-cultural impact to ensure that benefits are balanced and optimised while negative impacts are minimised. Impact evaluation should consider both the immediate resort site and its regional context. If negative impacts are unacceptable, the plan concept or configuration will need to be revised.

In maturing tourist destinations, it is often necessary to plan for controlled development, with a limit on the growth of tourism — and efforts to attract higher yield markets — so that economic benefits can be maintained without environmental and socio-cultural problems arising.

Planning for future demand growth

The resort planning should allow for flexibility of development, especially during the later stages of implementation, to allow for changing market trends and other influencing factors. But the basic concept of the resort and the integrity of its plan should still be maintained.

For larger resorts that are expected to be developed over a long period of time, the plan should be configured so that it can be developed in stages, with the earlier stages sufficiently self-contained for them to be efficiently managed and convenient for tourists to use before the later stages are developed.

Utilities

An adequate water supply, electric power, sewage and solid waste disposal and telecommunications, all designed to international standards, should be planned along with the land use planning. Where needed, the resort infrastructure should also be developed to serve local communities and thereby upgrade them.

Development and design standards

Development and design standards and guidelines, such as for densities, building heights and setbacks, percentage of open space and landscaping, parking, signage, general architectural styles and other elements, should be established as part of the planning and reflect the basic concept of the resort.

Leisure facilities

In response to current market trends and the increasing demand for all types of activities, a variety of recreation, cultural and leisure facilities and sight-seeing/activity-related attractions should be incorporated into the resort plan and into the tourism planning of the region in which the resort is located. In resort areas that are already developed, it may be necessary to expand and diversify such facilities and opportunities for tourist activities in order to maintain the resorts' viability.

Employee housing

Resort planning should consider relationships to any nearby communities and the provision of housing and community services for employees. In some places, new communities may need to be planned for resort employees and their families and, in other places, planning will be required for existing communities to absorb these employees.

IMPLEMENTATION AND MANAGEMENT

Implementation schedule

Careful and realistic programming or scheduling of the development of infrastructure and superstructure is essential, with every effort made to maintain this programme. If there is some delay in the programme, because of unforeseen circumstances which often arise, adjustments can be made to the scheduling. But the access and infrastructure must be available before the first accommodation is opened to tourists. Delays in development may increase costs but need not be a major deterrent to the ultimate success of the resort.

Effective organisation

An effective organisational structure, with experienced leadership and staff, is essential for successful implementation, financing and management of the resort. Often this organisation is a public corporation specifically set up to look after tourism development. Various types and levels of government agencies and public and private corporations are typically involved in the implementation process and coordination among these entities is essential. Coordination is typically the responsibility of the development authority. Private sector corporations increasingly assume some of these functions — but with government retaining control of planning and the application of development and design standards, so that the desired resort character and quality are maintained.

As development proceeds, the type of organisational structure may be changed so that the most suitable approach is applied at any particular time. The development and management responsibility is usually devolved from central to regional and local agencies as the latter gain experience in these functions. Whatever the type of organisational structure, it should be free from politically influenced decision-making.

Since it is often difficult to attract the initial or pioneer investors to a new resort, special provision may need to be made for the government or a public corporation to develop the first accommodation. Otherwise, substantial incentives should be provided to the private sector to attract this initial investment. An adequately financed and well directed investment promotion programme is also often required to attract private investors.

Land use development and design standards

Strict application of land use, development and designs standards must be maintained in order to achieve the desired type and quality level of the resort. Either government or the resort corporation is responsible for applying the development and design standards. These standards are often incorporated into legally enforceable zoning regulations (land use controls) written and adopted for

126

the resort. A procedure for reviewing and taking action on development proposals should be adopted by the governing authority and is often included in the zoning regulations.

If the local government is weak in applying development controls, the central government or development corporation must assume this responsibility until local government has become more experienced. A design review committee comprising design professionals is often organised to review and take action on site planning and the architectural design of proposed tourist facilities.

A decision needs to be made on whether to lease or sell the development sites to investors, and this will depend on local circumstances. Leasing gives more opportunity for the development authority, whether public or private, to maintain more long term control over the resort development, but it may be more difficult to obtain financing for facility development on leased sites.

Education and training

Adequate training of resort employees at all levels is essential for the successful operation of resorts, because the quality level of resorts and tourism generally depends very much on the quality of service provided. In addition to vocational and managerial education, language and cultural sensitivity training is important for employees in resorts that cater to guests of different cultural and language backgrounds. Provision for training, such as the development of a hotel and catering school, if needed, should be included in the resort development programme. Continuous upgrading, as well as the initial training, is an important part of an educational and training programme. If there are existing local communities, priority should be given to the training and employment of residents so that they receive this direct economic benefit from tourism development.

Regional planning implementation

The regional planning recommendations also need to be implemented, and this usually requires both the development of regional infrastructure and, in some cases, improvements to the infrastructure, facilities and services of local communities. It is also frequently necessary to apply local zoning regulations and development controls to the areas near the resort, in order to maintain their environmental quality without unduly restricting economic activities. Regional implementation may include the conservation and development of tourist attractions outside the resort as places to visit on day tours and to diversify opportunities for tourist activities in the general area.

Resort management

Effective resort management on a continuous basis is essential to maintain the character and quality of the resort and the infrastructure, and the infrastructure should be physically maintained to ensure its continued high level of operation.

Marketing the resort

Appropriate marketing of the resort to consumers and to tour operators who arrange group tours is essential, and major marketing efforts may be required during the early stages of the resort operation. An effective approach is often that of public and private sector cooperation on joint promotional programmes.

FINANCIAL CONSIDERATIONS

Identifying sources of funding

Infrastructure development is expensive and adequate funding must be provided for it. Infrastructure financing is typically secured through a combination of sources. These may include international and national/regional development banks, direct government investment and, in many cases, utility companies and agencies such as those for airport and highways. This funding, except perhaps from the utility and transportation agencies, can be channelled through the resort development corporation. If the infrastructure is multi-purpose, serving the general community as well as tourism needs, this helps justify funding the infrastructure required.

In some countries, national or regional development banks are established, either for general development purposes including tourism, or specifically for tourism projects. These development banks make loans, typically on a concessionary basis, that are not available from commercial banks. In addition, in countries with weak economies, international development bank financing for commercial development by the private sector may be available. In this situation, development bank loans should only be provided to developers whose proposals follow the resorts' land use plans, development controls and design standards.

Cooperation between the public and private sector financing source agencies is often important to organise the financing necessary, and imaginative financing techniques may need to be applied.

Recovering the costs

Much of the cost of developing the infrastructure can usually be recovered, and can be calculated to be recovered, through the increased value of development sites that are leased or sold to investors. For some types of infrastructure, such as water supply, electric power and sewage and solid waste disposal, payment of user fees by the commercial facilities can cover the operational costs and perhaps some of the capital investment costs. Permit fees may also be charged by the development authority to developers, to help defray infrastructure costs.

Higher taxes gained from the increased land value resulting from infrastructure development provides a source of indirect revenues that helps recover the investment costs. However, the initial development costs of infrastructure may not be recovered for several years and financing arrangements must be made to cover that interim period. Some of the regional infrastructure costs, such as for an airport or major highways, may need to be considered as a necessary government investment to encourage the overall economic growth of the region.

Attracting private sector investment

In order to attract private sector investment, special incentives or various types of tax exemptions may need to be offered. However, these incentives should be given only as long as they are needed and then reduced or eliminated, so that the government does not experience undue loss of revenue. Incentives should be offered only to those developers who agree to follow the land use plan, development controls and design standards established for the resort.

As already indicated, the government or public corporation may need to be the pioneer developer of commercial facilities. At a later date, however, when the resort has proved to be economically viable, these facilities can be sold to private companies.

A long term investment

Although not yet a serious problem in the case study resort areas reviewed in this report, there may be the tendency, as some resorts reach full development, to increase densities to gain short term profits. But this approach can lead to overdevelopment and loss of the resort's character and environmental quality, resulting in tourist dissatisfaction and marketing problems.

In addition, it may be found that the resort and its general area are not offering the types and diversity of tourist attractions and activities necessary to meet current market demands. It is therefore important that the resort quality be maintained through adherence to development controls but, at the same time, by adapting the facilities and services offered by the resort and its general area to meet changing market demands. Continuous effective resort management with monitoring of the resort's facilities, services, overall environmental quality, and its tourist market needs, is essential to maintain the resort's permanent viability.

Tourism and the Environment

Guidelines for Development of Parks and Protected Areas for Tourism is a newly published study outlining how to preserve the natural environment while maximizing the use of protected areas. The result of a joint project by the United Nations Environment Programme (UNEP) and the World Tourism Organization (WTO), the study suggests ways to balance the negative impacts tourism can have on protected areas with its social and economic benefits.

More specifically, The Guidelines provide park development and management plans for selecting and developing a park site, effectively staffing it, and finally marketing the park. It addresses "ecotourism" using environmentally conscious park development projects as examples. Projects that may serve as models for park preservation and sustainability into the 21st century.

The Guidelines for Development of Parks and Protected Areas for Tourism is available from the World Tourism Organization (WTO), Publications Unit, Capitan Haya 42, 28020 Madrid, Spain. The cost is US$ 35 plus air mail costs.

What is the WTO?

WTO, established in 1975 as the successor to the International Union of Official Travel Organizations (IUOTO), is the world's leading international organization in the field of travel and tourism. Its overall goal is the promotion and development of travel and tourism as a means of stimulating business and economic development, and fostering peace and understanding between nations.

WTO's membership comprises 113 of the world's governments and over 170 Affiliate Members from the travel and tourism industry. It is the only intergovernmental organization open to the operating sector. This combination of public and private sector involvement encourages a hands-on approach to strategic issues affecting the industry.

WTO's activities are divided into four major categories: technical cooperation, education and training, environment and planning, and facilitation and liberalization. It provides a forum for governments and industry to establish the frameworks and global standards of travel and tourism and thus the consolidation of one of the world's fastest growing industries.

Other WTO Publications:
- *Guidelines: Development of National Parks and Protected Areas for Tourism*
- *Sustainable Tourism Development: Guide for Local Planners*
- *Tourism Carrying Capacity*
- *Blue Flag Technical Manual*
- *Yearbook of Tourism Statistics*
- *Compendium of Tourism Statistics (annual)*
- *Travel and Tourism Barometer (quarterly)*

For more information, contact:
World Tourism Organization
Press and Publications
Capitán Haya, 42
28020 Madrid, Spain

Tel.: 341 - 571 - 0628
Fax: 341 - 571 - 3733

World Directory of Tourism Education and Training Institutions

WAPTT   AMFORT

A comprehensive global reference guide to over 700 institutions

CONTENTS

- **The Institution** - Name, legal status, address, telephone, fax and telex numbers.

- **General admission requirements** - Minimum age, entrance examination, professional experience.

- **Tourism education and training courses offered** - Qualifications for course admission, level and accreditation of degree or diploma granted, duration of courses, hours per week, fees for national and foreign students, practical training period.

- **Instructional support resources** - Specialized library, language laboratory, television and video equipment, computer equipment, training facilities in the areas of restaurant, hotel and travel agency.

- **Languages** - Main, compulsory and optional.

- **Financial Assistance** - Scholarships, other.

ALSO INCLUDED - *Special section* on **WTO** Education and Training Centres

World Directory of Tourism Education and Training Institutions is:

* Easy to consult

Convenient indexes and tables allow you to locate information swiftly and easily...

. by country
. by region
. by name of institution
. by title of diploma

* Comprehensive

A separate entry for each institution in English, French or Spanish containing the information you need.

* Reliable

The Directory is based on a worldwide survey of tourism education and training institutions, carried out by the **World Tourism Organization (WTO)** and the **World Association for Professional Training (WAPTT)**.

No hotel manager, student, educator, information centre or tourism professional should be without it!